CORNWALL
ARCHAEOLOGICAL
FROM PREHISTORY TO THE TUDORS:

Nicholas Johnson & Peter Rose
Cornwall Archaeological Unit
Cornwall County Council

INTRODUCTION

Archaeology is the study of our past through the material remains that are left behind; Cornwall is exceptionally rich in such evidence of its past. This is due largely to the use of stone for building and the relative isolation of Cornwall from intensive agricultural development. An astonishing range of monuments representing every period of history, single sites as well as relict landscapes can be found here. On Bodmin Moor, in West Penwith and on the Lizard are extensive remains of entire prehistoric farms as well as ritual and burial sites, medieval farms and early tinworks. It is not surprising therefore that there are more nationally designated protected monuments (Scheduled Monuments) in Cornwall than any other county in England. These precious reservoirs of information are often our only tangible link with our distant, and sometimes not so distant past and form an essential component of the Cornish landscape. This booklet is a brief guide to, and explanation of, the most accessible and representative examples of the archaeology of the county.

SITES NAMES FOLLOWED BY [G] WILL BE FOUND IN THE GAZETTEER SECTION

THE CHANGING LANDSCAPE

Since the end of the Ice Ages, approximately 10,000 years ago, Cornwall's landscape has undergone dramatic changes. At that time sea level was 37m (120 feet) lower than today with the shoreline in places up to four miles from the present coast. As the climate slowly warmed, a harsh arctic landscape gradually gave way to woodland. At the same time the melting ice caps caused the sea level to rise, engulfing wooded coastal lowlands. Many examples of such submerged forests are found around the coast when winter storms scour away the sand revealing tree roots and stumps. By the medieval period, the coastline was much as it is today but with the estuaries stretching far inland.

As the sea level rose so the coastal sand dunes advanced inland, covering Bronze Age and Iron Age settlements and burials. This loss of land continued in the medieval period with the

OPPOSITE PAGE *top:* The ancient landscape of West Penwith, at Bosigran, Zennor. Almost all the field boundaries are prehistoric in origin. A courtyard house hamlet lies in the middle of these fields.
below: Tintagel, post-Roman centre, with the later medieval castle.

overwhelming of settlements and churches at St Enodoc, Constantine Bay, Penhale Sands, Gwithian and the Hayle estuary.

Tin streaming in the medieval period led to extensive silting in many estuaries (the Hayle, Red River, Cober, Fal, Carnon, Fowey, Camel, Par and Tamar) and the consequent loss of Tregony, Lostwithiel, Grampound and Helston as ports. Post-medieval mining, quarrying and china clay extraction continued the burial or excavation of thousands of

hectares of landscape throughout the county. It is likely therefore that Cornwall has been shrunk, silted, buried and dug away more than any other area in Britain. All this has conspired to reduce and confuse the evidence for earlier communities. Thus, flint tools (the evidence for a camp of a hunting band) found in a ploughed field on the edge of the cliffs today, may have been several miles from the coast when the camp was originally in use.

Submerged forest, Mount's Bay   *Photo: Royal Institution of Cornwall collection*

Hunters and Gatherers
8000 – 4000BC MESOLITHIC PERIOD

Climate and vegetation changed rapidly after 8,000 BC. From cold grassland and patches of birch woodland, the fuller wildwood of oak and hazel with some elm and lime had developed by 6,000BC. Upland areas, even during the forest maximum, had only sparse tree cover with grassland covering the highest and most exposed parts.

Sometime after 5,500 BC Britain became separated from the continent by the rising sea; before this it was the north westernmost extremity of a land mass that stretched east to Siberia and south to the Mediterranean. Cornwall at that time fits into a general 'Southern English' tradition of semi-nomadic hunting bands. In winter they hunted amongst

the lowland woods, in summer, they followed the grazing herds onto their upland pastures; in spring they caught fish in the rivers and from boats at sea, and along the coast hunted seals and gathered crustaceans, shellfish, edible plants and seaweeds. Bushes and trees provided abundant berries, nuts and fruits in the summer and autumn. This was a way of life intimately bound up with the natural world: a world of woodland animals and birds, of the beaver, the red deer, wolf, bear and wild ox a world regulated by the seasons – campsites abandoned when the herds moved on or the fish run was over; shelters, perhaps tents o teepees, made from hide stitched togethe with sinew or gut; fires for roasting meat an hardening wooden points; sheltered hollows in which to make the tools and equipment so necessary to the hunter—armatures (arrow-heads, speartips etc) made from flint, fish spears from bone, and wood, nets from vegetable fibre, bags from skins, grinding stones for vegetable and dyestuff preparation; mocassins and clothes made from hard wearing but supple hides and skins. The raw materials were found close by; flint from beach pebbles around the coast, washed up from submarine chalk deposits (only rarely imported from South Devon and beyond); wood from the forest, skins and bone from the animals they hunted.

Towards 4,000 – 3,500 BC hunting bands began to use their environment more purpo-sefully; burning woodland to flush out game and encourage the growth of lush pasture; the partial domestication of animals, similar to the relationship that Laplanders' have with their reindeer today.

We have little physical evidence for this early period of Cornish prehistory, except for the scatters of imperishable flint and stone tools and waste flakes marking camp sites. The rising sea has covered many of the favoured coastal campsites, but in some areas (eg: around Gwithian, Trevose Head and the Padstow estuary) we can, through examining flint scatters in the ploughed fields, still catch a glimpse of a way of life familiar to us through early accounts of travellers amongst the Indians in North America.

Monuments of the first farmers
4000 – 2500BC NEOLITHIC PERIOD

Between 4,000 BC and 3,500 BC a new dimension in food provision was added to the already developing domestication of animals, namely farming:- the deliberate cultivation and harvesting of food plants. In many areas hunting continued to play a significant role, but by 2,000 BC this was in decline. Communities were now bound to the land they cultivated, and much of the history of the succeeding millennia is concerned with the creation of agricultural land and pasture, its maintenance, its allocation, and later its defence in the face of a steadily increasing population.

It is from this period that our first monuments have survived. Whilst it is known from flint scatters and other artefacts that settlements developed throughout the county there are no visible remains of these first farms to be seen today. As the heavily wooded landscape was increasingly cleared and farmed the growing population developed a social organisation and sense of territory that is reflected in their monuments. The massive 'megalithic' Chamber Tombs (Lanyon Quoit [G], Trethevy Quoit [G], Mulfra Quoit [G], Chun Quoit [G]) would have required the co-ordinated labour of a sizeable community. Generally known in Britain as 'Portal Dolmens' these monuments of the fourth millennium BC would have served as ritual foci and marked the community's ancestral territory. Slightly later (late fourth millennium) are the Long Cairns; these are rare in Cornwall (eg Lanyon Quoit [G], Woolley Barrow, SS 262 165).

Also in the fourth millennium tribal centres developed, perhaps controlling relatively large territories. At present two are known in Cornwall, at Helman Tor [G] and Carn Brea [G]. That at Carn Brea is an astonishing achievement for such an early date. A series of massive defensive ramparts enclose 46 acres. These ramparts take the form of a 2m wide and 2-3m high stone wall faced with upright stones back and front and stretch over at least 3,750m; no less than fifteen stone-lined entrances have been found.

During the Neolithic period there is good evidence from Cornwall of an extensive trade in objects of increasing sophistication, of the developing art of pottery and of polished stone axe production. By examining the mineralogical characteristics of these artefacts it has been possible to establish that much of the pottery of Cornwall for this period was made from clay originating on the Gabbro rock of the E Lizard; there were also at least 6 axe factories, sited where suitable igneous rock (often greenstone) could be easily exploited (eg St Just, Mount's Bay, SW of Camborne, W Hensbarrow, Balstone Down). Pottery and axes were distributed right across southern England. Axes were used for tree felling and wood-working but were clearly more significant than this: symbols of power and perhaps, magic, and were traded far and wide.

No farming settlements from this period have been located or excavated in Cornwall, but evidence from Carn Brea and elsewhere indicates that houses were rectangular. Fields,

cultivated with wooden stone-tipped hook ploughs (ards) or tipped hoes, began to have formal boundaries as a result of the never-ending struggle to clear them of stone, to keep the animals out, or pen them in.

Towards 2500 BC, henges, sites consisting of roughly circular areas enclosed by banks with internal ditches, were built across England. There are three in Cornwall—Castlewich SX 371685, Castilly SX 031628 and The Stripple Stones SX 143752. Their function is clearly not defensive and is assumed therefore to be social and ritual.

Carn Brea, Redruth. Neolithic and Iron Age hillfort encloses the area between the monument and castle.

Settlement and ceremony: an organised landscape
2500 – 600BC BRONZE AGE

Dividing up the past into manageable and meaningful units is an arbitrary process when new forms of tools, monuments and other artefacts were developing all the time. Although the introduction of metalworking is an important cultural marker it was not for many hundreds of years (not until c1400 BC) that bronze was used for everyday tools and weapons, rather than being a rare metal used by an elite for objects of prestige and display. A more significant break occurs earlier in prehistory; the appearance of henges in the late Neolithic sees the beginning of a tradition of ceremonial monuments which stretches without a break through the Early Bronze Age. At first gold and then copper objects were made, but increasingly bronze (made by the alloying of tin and lead with copper) became the material most used for metal artefacts. During those early days (before 2000 BC) there is stylistic evidence for close contact and

trade with Ireland. Four gold lunulae (crescentic collars) found in Cornwall are of Irish design but made from Cornish gold. It is likely that Cornish sources of tin, copper and perhaps lead were used even at this early date—the tin lying as heavy black pebbles in many streams and copper clearly visible as a green streak on

Early Bronze Age lunulae.

The Merry Maidens stone circle

rock outcrops and cliffs. The discovery of early artefacts within the tin gravels takes the tin industry back to prehistory. Over the succeeding centuries, technological advances allowed metalwork styles to evolve from flat axes (made in single moulds) to more complex weapons and tools (made in two-sided moulds) and sophisticated bronze jewellery. The late Neolithic and Early Bronze Age (c2500 – 1400 BC) is characterised by its ceremonial and burial monuments, the stone circles, stone rows, standing stones (menhirs) and barrows or cairns. A local variant of barrows, the entrance graves are found in Penwith and on Scilly where they may have originated. A kerbed stone mound contains a simple passage or chamber of drystone construction capped with massive slabs. Whilst not as sophisticated as Stonehenge, the Cornish circles are nonetheless beautiful and evocative (Merry Maidens [G], Tregeseal, Fernacre [G-72], Trippet stones [G], the Hurlers [G]). They are best interpreted as places for the public performance of ceremonial and ritual. Even more enigmatic are the stone rows, though their form hints at use in processions; they are straight alignments of stones, usually either all large or all small, some closely, some widely spaced. These, with Standing Stones (Menhirs) were originally much more widespread, and as with stone circles they survive today largely in upland areas. (Stone Rows:- seven on Bodmin Moor, and the Nine Maidens [G] on St Breock Downs. Standing Stones:- many in West Penwith eg: Goon Rith [G-52] and on Bodmin Moor eg: The Pipers [G-54]. The standing stones were probably marker stones: the burials sometimes found by them suggesting that they were memorial stones, grave markers, way markers or territorial boundary stones.

We get our best glimpse of Bronze Age life and death on Bodmin Moor, on the Lizard, and in West Penwith. During the 2nd millennium BC these areas were densely settled (eg: Roughtor area [G], Stowe's Pound areas [G-54]). The foundations of hundreds of stone round houses and many hundreds of acres of fields, now defined by low stone banks, lie scattered across these upland plateaux and valley sides. Some appear to be permanently occupied settlements, complete with fields, but others may have been used only seasonally during summer grazing of the uplands. Associated with them are stone circles, standing stones, stone rows, and the barrows and cairns (the former being mounds of earth, the latter of stone). In some parts of Britain these are first and foremost burial mounds, but in Cornwall excavation has shown them to be complex and varied sites where burial was only one of the rites performed; many do not have burials at all. Most date from the period 2000 to 1600 BC. The variety in size and shape is remarkable. Diameters range from 2m to 40m. Some are simple mounds of earth, turf or stone; others have a revetting wall or kerb; some incorporate a

One of the enigmatic holed stones, thought to be Early Bronze Age. Kenidjack, St Just in Penwith

Bronze Age burial cist, Bodmin Moor

natural outcrop or tor, and a few are doughnut-shaped 'ring-cairns'. Many have a stone burial box (cist) as a component. The dead were usually cremated and the ashes buried in an urn, sometimes with other personal objects such as beads, a dagger, or a bone ornament such as a pin or archers' wrist brace. Some mounds are probably burials of important people. The largest barrows are in prominent locations on hilltops and ridges. The smaller barrows, which do not normally survive in lowland Cornwall, are inconspicuously sited amongst the fields and near the contemporary settlements. It is only in these upland areas that it is possible to examine the spatial and chronological relationships between the settlements, burials and ritual monuments in their contemporary setting. We can conclude that the many barrows found elsewhere in lowland Cornwall (eg: Cubert Common,

SW 7810 5945, Veryan Beacon) would have had round house settlements close by which are not now visible. In looking at the area around Roughtor [G] we are looking at the upper edges of a 3,000 year old farming landscape which has elsewhere in the lowland Cornwall now been largely ploughed away. These farms consist of large curvilinear fields attached or accreted on to each other with round houses accessible via trackways through the fields. They are usually separated from their neighbours by open areas of common grazing or perhaps woodland. As the population increased so farms began to crowd closer together. There is evidence that at some time after 1700 BC there was a pressing need for a more systematic organisation of the landscape. On Dartmoor this took the form of Reave systems where very large areas were subdivided by a regular pattern of fields and major pastoral boundaries. On Bodmin Moor, grazing blocks were defined by substantial stone boundaries, and in Penwith and probably over much of the rest of lowland Cornwall the countryside was divided into regular small arable fields. The rectilinear net-like field systems laid out during this period underlie the modern field pattern of parts of the northern part of West Penwith (see inside front cover). The pastoral boundaries on Bodmin Moor may indicate that, after a widespread early attempt at arable farming, soil degradation and deteriorating climate necessitated a change to seasonal grazing and less intensive exploitation. Permanent settlement retreated to the moorland edges and the lowlands but clusters of moorland round houses were still used for seasonal grazing.

A typical Bronze Age barrow

Bronze Age round house on Bodmin Moor

It is difficult to imagine what society must have been like but in the Early Bronze Age it seems certain that religion and ceremony were inseparably woven into the fabric of everyday life. At the same time, the presence of an elite or aristocracy is indicated by individual burials with prestigious grave goods of display and rank, such as daggers, and jewellery of amber and faience glass. Weaponry is present throughout, but the apparent disappearance of the bow (by c1500 BC) may reflect a greater emphasis on individual combat. In addition, Cornwall has several defended enclosures that may date from the early part of this period (Roughtor [G], Stowe's Pound [G-54]). Pottery styles change throughout the period with many new types of decoration and shapes. Most of this material comes from burials and is recovered through excavation of the mounds. Houses, whether built in stone or wood, were round, and often have evidence of internal compartments and central hearths and bear the traces of indoor activities such as weaving. Wooden rafters supported thatched roofs. Many had an internal capacity as large or larger

than a typical Cornish 19th century one up one down cottage.

Excavations of Bronze Age fields buried by sand at Gwithian (SW 5900 4220) showed evidence of scratch marks in the sub soil made by the hook-shaped ploughs as well as marks around the field edges made by spade digging in those areas the plough could not reach. The farming calendar and activities for most of the population in the Bronze Age cannot have been dramatically different to that known to the Cornish peasant farmer only 150 years ago. By the 1st millennium BC the megalithic ritual monuments (standing stones, stone rows, stone circles) had long since been abandoned, the uplands, now largely moorland, had been turned over to seasonal grazing. As yet the centuries from c1200 – 400 BC are very obscure because of the lack of obvious ritual monuments or defended sites but this is likely to have been an important formative period during which the lowlands were increasingly being opened up to permanent farming.

A Bronze Age urn

Farmers and Fighters – A Celtic Society
600BC – AD43 IRON AGE

Iron gradually replaced bronze for the weapons of fighting and tools for farming during the 7th century BC. It is possible that iron deposits found in Cornwall were exploited at this early date (Trevelgue [G]). In Cornwall more significant cultural and social changes may have occurred both before and after the adoption of iron, which is not now thought to

have been introduced by invaders; pottery styles changed completely in the Later Bronze Age, and hillforts and defended farmsteads were not widely constructed until the fourth century BC.

It is these defended sites which characterise the period, though unenclosed settlements of round houses and fields may always have been

Warbstow Bury hillfort

Iron Age defended farmstead, Pennance, Camborne, still clearly defined partly by a curved hedge and partly as a cropmark

equally common; these however have been obliterated by 2000 years of continuing agricultural activity.

The hillforts were defended by substantial earth, rubble or stone ramparts topped by wooden palisades or stone walls and had deep, sometimes rock cut, ditches. Fortified gateways through the formidable defences gave access to well organised permanent settlements of round houses; evidence of metalworking is sometimes found. (Castle an Dinas [G], Castle Dore [G], Warbstow Bury [G], St Dennis [G], Helsbury [G]). Similar sites known as cliff castles were sited on coastal promontories or headlands; these are often in very exposed locations and some may have been only temporary refuges. (Mayon [G], Treryn Dinas [G], Gurnard's Head [G], Rame Head [G], Trevelgue [G], The Dodman [G]). Another variation of the hillfort is the 'multiple enclosure', with either an annexe or a series of widely spaced ramparts, thought to be for the corralling of cattle.

The strongly defended hillforts, cliff castles and

multiple enclosures were economic and social centres, the fortresses of the aristocracy or tribal chiefs who wielded considerable power over the surrounding countryside, their wealth perhaps expressed in cattle, their position bolstered by tribute from the surrounding farmers. Classical authors portray the Celts as dominated by a warrior aristocracy fond of fighting, feasting and boasting and incapable of concerted action. The sheer number of hillforts in Cornwall (over 80) seems to tell the same story.

Contrasting with these strongly defended sites are the 'rounds', farmsteads and hamlets defended by a single rampart and found not on hilltops but on hillslopes and spurs in generally favoured farmland. Hundreds are known throughout Cornwall. Found at a few settlements in West Cornwall are the mysterious stone-built tunnels known as 'fogous' (Cornish for 'cave'; eg Carn Euny [G], Halligye [G]). Examples found in Rounds (eg Halligye) may have an exit running out beneath the rampart. This lends credence to the theory that they were used as temporary refuges during brief onslaughts by raiding parties, but a case can also be made for use as cold stores (eg for dairy products) or as structures used for religious purposes.

Burial was in cemeteries of pit-graves, sometimes lined with stone, with the dead placed on their side in a crouched position, and normally aligned north-south. Little is found with them, usually just the brooch that fastened their clothes.

Iron Age bronze mirror. Found with a burial at Trelan, St Keverne

Under New Management
AD43 – AD410 ROMANO-BRITISH PERIOD

We must imagine a rural society over large parts of lowland Cornwall, ruled over by a fractious aristocracy. For many decades before the Roman invasion Cornwall must have received its share of Gaulish refugees with tales of hardship under the Roman yoke but for some the arrival of the Romans may have been a godsend — Celtic chiefs who saw the chance to gain an advantage over other tribal groups, traders anxious to exploit the commercial opportunities of becoming part of an Empire that stretched to Egypt and beyond. It appears that many of the larger hillforts were already abandoned by the time the Roman legions marched west. Following the subjugation of the southern tribes, the Second Augustan Legion built and occupied the fortress at Exeter (ISCA DUMNONIORUM) between AD55 – 75. Presumably up until then the Dumnonii had not posed any threat. Whatever caused the Romans to extend the frontier zone into Cornwall, the results were not as dramatic as elsewhere in Britain. So far only one fort, that at Nanstallon (SX 046670), is known. It is sited close to the then navigable River Camel and could therefore have access both to the

sea and to the ridgeway along the high ground between the Camel and Fowey rivers — a routeway dominated in previous centuries by the enormous hillfort of Castle Canyke (SX 086658 -overlooking the Bodmin-Liskeard roundabout on the Bodmin bypass).

Cornwall was incorporated into the administrative area or 'civitas' centred on Exeter. It appears that many hillforts were forcibly abandoned during the military occupation but what is equally clear is that most important rounds were not; they were probably left in the hands of client or trusted chiefs. Large enclosures or rounds such as Carvossa (SW 919483) in the Fal Valley and Carloggas, St Mawgan (SW 873653) continued in occupation and excavation has produced a wide range of typical Roman artefacts, Gaulish Samian ware, glass and metalwork. Elsewhere rounds continued to be built although a sub-rectangular shape was often preferred. Excavation has shown that during the Roman period the shape of houses changed from circular to oval or elongated, perhaps influenced by Roman building practice. However, the main agents for Romanisation are not found in Cornwall;

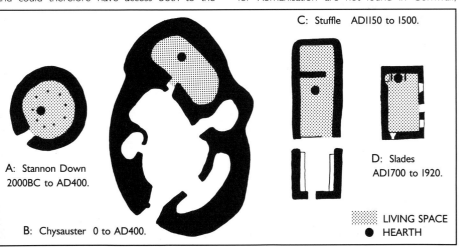

C: Stuffle   ADII50 to I500.

A: Stannon Down
2000BC to AD400.

D: Slades
AD1700 to 1920.

B: Chysauster 0 to AD400.

LIVING SPACE
● HEARTH

Average living space, 2000BC to AD1900:
A: Bronze Age round house, 33m^2; B: Courtyard house, 32m^2; C: Longhouse, 35m^2; D: Cottage (two stories), 40-45m^2

there are no towns and only one or two villas. Rural life no doubt continued much as before and even though power had shifted decisively to the invader, it is likely that, apart from a few Roman administrators, Roman Cornwall was still ruled by the pre-invasion tribal leaders and their descendants.

A form of settlement not found elsewhere in Britain developed in west Cornwall and the Isles of Scilly in the 2nd century AD. Courtyard Houses consist of round and oval stone dwellings, sub rectangular byres and other farm buildings that look onto open, partially paved, farm yards (courtyard). The structures are confined within massive stone walls with substantial gates giving access to the yard. Each unit represents a self-contained farmhouse. Over thirty courtyard house settlements are known. They vary from substantial hamlets as at Chysauster [G] to single units. Many developed from open settlements of round houses, and their fields, by then already many centuries old, continued to be used. By the end of the 5th century AD the area under cultivation along the north coast of Penwith cannot have been much different from the area cultivated only 150 years ago. The constant clearing of stones and the relentless movement of ploughsoil downhill during this period, and over the succeeding centuries, has ensured

that the massively walled fields survive and today they are a vital part of this uniquely beautiful and ancient landscape. It is likely that the fields here have been in use since at least the Iron Age, over 2000 years ago.

Tin became important after the 2nd century AD when the Empire's Iberian mines were in decline. Used in coins and pewter ware, tin was transported from the tin gravel extraction sites to the markets in ingot form. Many ingots of this date are known from Cornwall and it is likely that, as with other mineral producing areas, Cornish tin was worked under Imperial control.

By the time the last legions were withdrawn from Britain in AD410 for the defence of the Roman heartland, Cornish society had changed. There was a monetary economy where none had existed before, trading links had been extended, farming had undoubtedly expanded and finds of fine wares, coin hoards and expensive high status metalwork suggest that, though unsophisticated by Roman provincial standards, Cornwall was by no means impoverished. Many people had no doubt adopted Roman names, manners and accents but it was not long before society began to splinter; Cornwall was still, despite 350 years of Roman bureaucracy, essentially Celtic in character.

Chysauster courtyard house settlement

Cornish Kings and Celtic Saints
AD410 – 1066 EARLY MEDIEVAL PERIOD

From the 5th century, after Rome had abandoned its peripheral areas, Britain fragmented into a series of kingdoms, British in the west, Anglo-Saxon in the east. A handful of Dumnonian kings are known by name — Constantine in the 6th century, Gereint in the 8th, Dumgarth in the 9th — but most are unrecorded or are lost in myth.

This obscure period saw considerable movement of peoples; as well as the migrations of the Anglo-Saxons, the Irish crossed to Scotland and Wales and their presence is attested in Cornwall by Irish names and the use of the ogham script on early Christian inscribed stones (eg: Lewannick [G]). At the same time, a British migration to NW France was effected on such a scale that from the mid 6th century Armorica was known as Britannia or Brittany. The names of two Breton regions, Dumnonia and Cornouaille, point to the source of this migration, and continuing contact is shown in the traditions of the Cornish and Breton saints, and in a shared language, indistinguishable before the 8th century.

The sporadic conquest of the 'West Welsh' (Cornish) by the armies of the Kings of Wessex was under way by 710 when Gereint was obliged to cede territory in SE Cornwall, but this was followed in 722 by a Cornish victory. Egbert's campaigns in the 9th century, culminating in 838 in the defeat of a combined Cornish and Danish army at Hingston Down, left Cornwall a vassal kingdom. But only in the extreme SE and NE of Cornwall are there concentrations of English place-names, suggesting that actual English colonisation was on a small scale. Two Linear Earthworks, the Bolster Bank, St Agnes (still partly visible as a rampart between Trevaunance Cove and Chapel Coombe) and the Giant's Hedge (originally stretching between Lerryn and Looe, substantial sections of which are visible north of Lanreath), may have been territorial defences of the early part of this period.

The key archaeological site of this period is Tintagel [G], which is now thought to be a royal stronghold of the early 6th century. The occupation can be dated by large quantities of pottery, both storage vessels (amphorae) and fine wares, imported from the Mediterranean, an indication of western Britain's continuing cultural and economic links with Byzantium. At the same time there is a little evidence for the reoccupation of Iron Age hillforts (Chun [G] is the only good example), perhaps by the local aristocracy. Other important places are suggested by the place-name **lis**, 'hall' or 'court', eg Liskeard, Lesnewth, Lizard, Lesingey.

By the time of the Norman conquest the Cornish countryside was quite thickly populated. This is clear not so much from Domesday Book as from the place-name evidence. Places with the elements **tre** (estate, farm, or hamlet) or **bod** (dwelling), indicative of settlements of pre-Norman origin, are found in profusion throughout Cornwall and many may originate in the 7th century or before. Many other settlements with Cornish place-names are likely to be equally ancient; the pattern of settlements found in medieval Cornwall (and later) is almost entirely pre-Norman in origin. Just how far back this pattern goes has yet to be established; there was an, as yet, unexplained change, sometime between the 4th and 7th

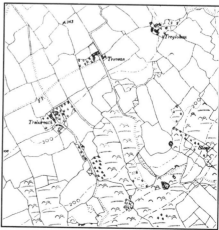

Farms, fields and lanes of early medieval origin on the Lizard

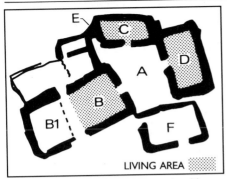

One of the farm complexes excavated at Mawgan Porth:
A: courtyard;   B: longhouse with byre (B1);
C & D: houses with hearths and box-beds;
E: kennel?   F: outbuildings.
The longhouse measures 10m (32') internally.

centuries when the rounds were abandoned in favour of the undefended, open settlements which became the predominant type.

Very little is known from archaeological excavation about the character of these early settlements. Excavated sites of the 5th and 6th centuries are mostly of Romano-British origin, such as the round at Trethurgy with its oval houses. Most pre-Norman farms have continued in use to the present day but one settlement of the 10th and 11th centuries, buried beneath the sand at Mawgan Porth (SW 8520 6730), was found on excavation to be a hamlet of rectangular houses, and is a forerunner of the typical later medieval hamlets.

If most of Cornwall's farms are probably of pre-Norman origin the same is likely to be true of the lanes and tracks that link them, and many of our Cornish hedges may be on the line of early field boundaries. The general pattern of land use found in the medieval period and later is also an early feature. In most cases each farm or hamlet would have had access to an area of rough grazing, usually on higher ground, but this pattern has mostly been obscured by the enclosures of the 19th century and earlier.

A major force for change, in the 5th and 6th centuries, was the introduction of Christianity from Wales, the Mediterranean and Gaul. The earliest religious communities (or monasteries)

took the form of enclosed settlements not unlike the contemporary rounds. Known as lanns, these would have contained a chapel, a burial ground and a few houses. The form of these enclosures can still be seen in the outline of many churchyards (eg: St Buryan [G]). These communities were supported by endowments of land, which in some cases (eg St Petroc's of Padstow and Bodmin) became very considerable. But by 1086 most had dwindled or disappeared as their estates were seized first by the English (Anglo-Saxons) and then by the Normans.

Inscribed stones, commemorating important individuals of the 5th to 7th centuries, were set up in some lanns but also beside tracks and fords (eg: Lewannick [G], St Clement [G]). The names on the stones reflect the mixed cultural influences of the time — Irish, British and Latin names all occur, some inter-mixed: the stone in St Kew church is inscribed IVSTI (Latin: 'the stone of Justus') but the name is repeated in Ogham, the Irish stroke alphabet.

The earliest Cornish crosses, finely ornamented with interlace designs, date from the late 9th century and served both as memorials and as churchyard crosses. Fine examples can be seen at St Neot [G], Sancreed [G] and Cardinham [G]. The Doniert Stone [G] was probably erected by Dumgarth, the last Cornish king to be recorded, who drowned in 875.

By the 10th and 11th centuries many more religious sites had been established. Important manors had their own chapels and every small group of hamlets would have had its own burial ground, such as at Mawgan Porth, or Merther Euny in Wendron (SW 704294), where an abandoned Romano-British round was re-used. As the parochial system developed some of these cemeteries acquired a parish church, but many others went out of use.

Old pagan beliefs may have been assimilated as well as ousted by the spread of Christianity. This is suggested by the large number of holy wells. Most have medieval superstructures but their supposed supernatural powers may well have pre-Christian origins.

Tin, fish and farming – a broad economy
AD 1066 – 1540 MEDIEVAL PERIOD

The Norman Conquest saw the complete replacement of one ruling elite by another. By the time of Domesday Book (1086) only 67 poor manors were held by Anglo-Saxons (English) and these were held not directly but from Norman overlords. Robert of Mortain, the Conqueror's half brother, held 277 of the 350 Cornish manors; as well as displacing the English he dispossessed several of the ancient Cornish religious houses such as at St Neot and St Kew. Wealth and power resided in the holding of land; the Normans secured what they had taken with a series of formidable and intimidating castles. Robert had castles at Launceston [G] and Trematon (SX 411579). Others belonged to his chief sub-tenants, as at Cardinham [G], Week St Mary [G] and Restormel [G].

The castles of the 11th and 12th centuries are either of motte and bailey type, as at Launceston [G], Trematon near Saltash, Cardinham [G] and Kilkhampton [G], or are 'ringworks' where the principal stronghold is a simple bank and ditch that would have contained a building or two (Upton Castle, Bossiney Castle).

From the 13th century the major castles, Launceston SX 246789, Trematon, Restormel SX 065 888 [G] and Tintagel [G], now in the hands of the Earls and then the Dukes of Cornwall, were allowed to slide into decay; they were remote from the heartland of medieval politics where the Earls and Dukes actually resided.

In the 13th and 14th centuries some of the leading Cornish families provided their residences with some form of defence. Little now survives of these sites; a broad, deep moat may still be seen at Binhany, Stratton (SS 219 058), the home of the Blanchminsters, though the buildings within are reduced to amorphous mounds. At Berry Court, Jacobstow [G], the layout of the moated manor has been revealed by excavation.

As in other parts of Britain the 11th to 14th centuries was a period of economic and

Launceston Castle

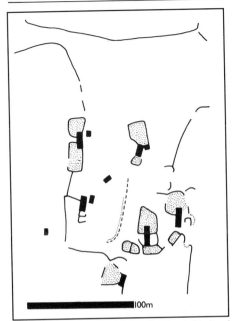

Lamlavery, Davidstow Moor. Deserted Medieval hamlet.

population growth resulting in the development of Open Field systems, and the appearance of many small towns. In addition Cornwall had the basis for a very diverse economy with the development of trade, fishing, quarrying, the cloth industry and especially the tin industry.

By the early 14th century Cornwall would have been more densely populated than ever before. The county was already thickly covered with farms and hamlets at the time of the Norman Conquest and so the pressure on available land led to the colonisation of upland areas like Bodmin Moor as well as the growth and subdivision of existing hamlets.

After the Black Death of 1349 many of the hamlets on Bodmin Moor were abandoned as people took up holdings that had become available on better land off the moor; these deserted sites are our best evidence for the form of medieval settlements. Most are hamlets, with from two to six farmhouses, though those in lowland Cornwall would have been rather larger.

In Cornwall medieval houses very rarely survive in use and those that do tend to be the

grander examples (eg: Cotehele [G]). Typical peasants' houses are best known from excavation. These were normally 'long-houses', which provided accommodation for the family and for the wintering of stock under the same roof, but separated by a cross passage (eg: Lamlavery [G], Louden [G-72]).

In the 13th and early 14th centuries most hamlets would have been surrounded by arable fields divided into strips — the local version of the open field system. These survive best on Bodmin Moor where the strips are divided by low banks of stone. As pressure on land was eased after the Black Death, holdings became amalgamated and blocks of strips were enclosed, sometimes preserving the strip-like pattern. A few open-field systems continued in use to the 19th century and one can still be seen at Boscastle — the Forrabury Stitches.

Although Cornwall was essentially rural in character, by the 14th century it was well served by a network of towns and markets. Only on the Lizard and on Bodmin Moor would country folk have had to travel more than six or seven miles to market. There has been virtually no archaeological excavation to examine the character of early Cornish towns, and only very rarely do medieval buildings

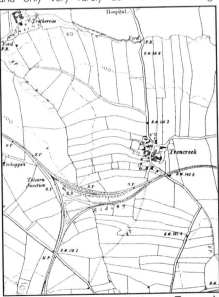

Fossilised medieval strip fields at Trencreek, St Columb Minor. 1907 Ordnance Survey

Unique in Cornwall, the survival of a strip field system in use, at Forrabury, Boscastle

survive, but in most cases the original layout of the towns, the pattern of streets and house plots, can still be seen. Only Launceston [G] was deemed important enough to have a town wall; the South Gate remains intact. Most market towns were set up by local landowners as a profitable source of revenue.

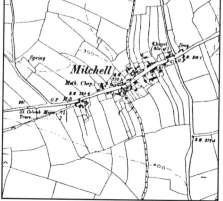

Layout of burgage plots in the small medieval town and notorious Rottten Borough of Mitchell,

Some like Week St Mary [G] or Mitchell were scarcely more than villages and would have provided local farms and hamlets with basic commodities and a market for their produce. Others like Bodmin [G] or Lostwithiel [G] would have had populations of a few thousand and a wide range of craft specialists. Some towns were located on spine roads and routeways (eg Mitchell, Grampound, Camelford and Wadebridge) but most had connections with the sea, as fishing ports, trading ports or both. In addition to coastal trade, Cornwall exported tin, fish, slate and cloth and imported salt, linen and canvas from Brittany, white fish, cloaks and wood from Ireland, wine from France, wine and fruit from Spain. Smuggling and piracy were traditional supplements to fair trading. Piracy, of course, could also be a grave threat. There are numerous records of fishermen from Cornwall being taken by barbary pirates.

Medieval Cornwall was remarkable for its diverse economy, based on a wide range of industries which involved thousands of people. The tinners and fishermen were pre-eminent

Medieval dovecote, Trevannion, Wadebridge

but wool cloth manufacture, quarrying and ship building also grew in importance. Quarries such as those at Pentewan, Polyphant and Cataclews provided building stone on a local basis, but roofing slates had a wider market and were quarried (eg: Tintagel and Delabole) and exported from the end of the 12th century, for example to Dover and Southampton.

The tin industry had its own laws and privileges and the Stannary Courts (Lostwithiel [G]) administered justice in the four stannaries or tin producing areas — Penwith/Kerrier; Tywarnhayle (St Agnes); Blackmore (St Austell); Foweymore (Bodmin Moor). At this date most of the tin would have been dug from the valley gravels, into which tin ore, weathered and eroded from the lodes or veins, had been redeposited. The earthworks resulting from the systematic digging over of these deposits can still be seen as streamworks in some of the valleys on Bodmin Moor. During the 13 – 16th centuries the centre of tin production shifted from the streamwork-dominated eastern stannaries to the west where opencast and shallow underground mining was more common. The ore was crushed in water-powered crazing and stamping mills and the tin smelted in blowing houses. Twice a year the ingots were taken to the 'Coinage Towns' (Liskeard, Lostwithiel [G] Truro and Helston) to be assayed. To check the purity, the corner of the ingot was removed; the term 'coinage' is derived from quoin, French for corner. Then it was taxed before sale to national and international markets, mostly for the manufacture of pewter. There developed, inevitably, a strong tradition of smuggling untaxed tin abroad.

It is difficult now to appreciate the importance of the Church in medieval Cornwall and its central place in everyday life. For example, in 16th century Bodmin [G] in addition to the

A pre-Norman church site, in its original circular graveyard, at St Mabyn

priory, friary, parish church, five chapels, two hospitals and two leper hospitals, a large proportion of the forty guilds were religious or charitable associations. Throughout Cornwall there was a profusion of chapels (eg: Roche rock [G], Madron [G]), holy wells (eg: Dupath [G], St Cleer [G]) and crosses (eg: St Cleer [G]) and important places of pilgrimage (eg: St Michael's Mount [G]).

On the other hand, Cornwall's religious houses were mostly on a small scale; there were no abbeys, for example. St Germans [G] and St Michael's Mount [G] are the most complete survivals of priory churches, but fragments can also be seen at St Thomas' Launceston [G] and at Bodmin [G].

Many of the parish churches are on sites that have been in use for worship since the 5th or 6th centuries. Most were extensively rebuilt in the 15th century, though many retain traces of 12th and 13th century architecture; fine Norman fonts are often a feature of Cornish churches.

Very little survives of the 700 or so medieval chapels. Some were of pre-Norman origin but most were private chapels attached to the houses of the gentry (eg Cotehele [G] or Trecarrell). Others served a more public function, standing by bridges or fords or acting as a lighthouse or daymark (St Ives and Rame Head [G]. Perhaps best known of all is the chapel at Roche Rock [G], served by a hermit.

A particular characteristic of Cornwall is its wealth of granite crosses. Most are wayside crosses, marking the path to church, but some were set up as churchyard crosses, including the more ornate 'lantern' crosses which depict biblical scenes on their heads (St Neot [G]).

By the mid-16th century Cornwall was relatively prosperous, but still very much a county with a distinctive identity. Cornish was still spoken widely in the west and communications with the rest of England were by sea or along difficult and often dangerous roads. The period closes with the Reformation, and the suppression of very many religious houses. Cornwall was a major area of rebellion against the changes brought about by the split from Rome. At the same time it was moving to the centre of the stage regarding the defence of England against France and then Spain.

A Medieval wayside cross near Madron Holy Well

GAZETTEER

The sites in this gazetteer have been chosen as representative of all periods, well preserved, and freely and easily accessible. There are hundreds of others that could have been included and many of these are marked on Ordnance Survey maps. The details given for each monument should help anyone to recognise the purpose and significance of such sites as well as others that have not been included.

The gazetteer has been arranged in alphabetical order, with the Saint prefix in place names ignored; St Breock is therefore to be found under B not S. National Grid references are given so sites may easily be located with the OS Landranger (1:50,000) map series. Details of how to get there are only included if there may be some difficulty in finding the site.

The following shorthand information is given with each entry.

NG grid reference: SX 203686   Name of site on map: (Caer Vallack)

Ownership of site:

NT — National Trust	EH — English Heritage	CHT — Cornwall Heritage Trust
LA — Local Authority	PC — Parish Council	

Parking space(s) available close by: [P]   Public footpath to site: Foot   Guide book available: GD
Walking more than 100m necessary: Walk   Good view from site: View

IMPORTANT: When visiting these sites abide by the Country Code: When in doubt always ask permission: Report any damage immediately to Cornwall Archaeological Unit, Tel: Truro (0872) 74282 ext 3603.

1 BERRY COURT (PENHALLAM)

EH [P] Walk   SX 224974

Down a farm road to the S of the road from Jacobstow to Week St Mary. The remains of a moated manor house of the 12—13th centuries. Built by the Cardinham family and occupied until the 14th century, it comprises the footings of a range of buildings built around a courtyard and approached through a gatehouse with a drawbridge over the moat. As well as the Hall and Chapel there were the lord's as well as guest's lodgings, and a large kitchen range rebuilt after a fire c1300.

2 BODMIN

Town, Church, Chantry, Well and Priory

[P] GD   SX 073670

The largest of Cornwall's medieval towns, consisting of one long street which at the E focussed on the Priory and the parish church. The town was in existence by the 10th century and is recorded in Domesday Book, having grown up around Cornwall's most important monastery, St Petroc's (having moved from Padstow following a Viking raid). This was probably on the site of the present parish church, the largest in Cornwall, which is predominantly 15th century and has a splendid Norman font. The 12th century Bodmin Casket, St Petroc's reliquary, is displayed in the S aisle. In the churchyard is St Guron's Well, a small 16th century structure and a Chantry Chapel built in 1377 and dedicated to St Thomas Becket. It has a beautiful east window and a porch gives access to a crypt. After the Dissolution the chapel served as a grammar school from 1566 to 1853 and the crypt was used as a charnel house.

The ancient monastery was re-established nearby at the beginning of the 12th century as the Augustinian Priory of St Mary the Virgin and St Petroc and the original monastery church given over as the parish church. Following the Dissolution the buildings were re-used and demolished over 200 years.

Excavations in 1984 revealed the foundations of the NW corner of the church, which would have been similar in size and appearance to that at St Germans [G]. The foundations may be seen in the grounds of Priory House, opposite the church. The cloisters stood between the priory church and the priory fish pond to the S.

3 BOSCAWEN UN (NINE MAIDENS)
Stone Circle
Walk Foot   SW 412274 (Stone circle)
Reached by the lane from Boscawen-noon farm or a path from the A30, this circle is particularly well preserved. The stones were restored in 1862 when a bisecting hedge was removed. In a late medieval work the site is named as one of the three main Druidic meeting places in Britain. Stone circles, built nearly 1500 years before the Druids, are often, erroneously, linked to them.

4 BREAGE
Church, Wall painting, Cross, Roman milestone
[P] GD   SW 618285 (Church)
The 15th century church contains well preserved medieval wall paintings of St Christopher, Christ of the Trades survive and other saints. Within the church is a Roman milestone inscribed in latin shorthand to 'the Emperor Caesar our lord Marcus Cassianus Latinius Postumus, pious, fortunate, august'. It is the only surviving stone dedicated to Postumus (AD 258 – 268) to survive in Britain. He was a usurper who ruled only part of the empire (Britain, Gaul and Spain). Another milestone can be seen in St Hilary church (SW 551313) and with Breage marks the old route to the Land's End peninsula and Mount's Bay.

5 ST BREOCK LONGSTONE
Standing stone
EH [P]
SW 968683 (Longstone)
Known as Men Gurta, it is the heaviest standing stone still upright. Having fallen in 1945, it was re-erected in 1956. It stands within a low mound of quartz stones. 900m to the E is another standing stone. There are over 90 barrows along St Breock Downs from the Camel Valley to St Eval. The best survive in moorland on either side of A39 to the north of the Nine Maidens stone row [G].

6 ST BURYAN
Church, Crosses
[P]   SW 409257 (Church)
Circular churchyard found, by excavation, to be within an Iron Age/Romano-British earthwork (probably an enclosed farm). Traditionally founded by King Athelstan in the 10th century it became a collegiate church in 13th century; mostly now 15th century. Outside the main churchyard entrance is a small cross on a massive base carved with a figure of Christ on one side and a cross on the other. The churchyard cross lies near the porch and is also on a massive stepped base. It has a fine four holed head with a raised carving of Christ on an elaborate cross; probably carved by RUNHOL the sculptor of crosses at Sancreed [G] and St Mawgan (SW 872658) in the 10th century.

7 CADSONBURY
Hillfort
NT Foot Walk [P]   SX 344673 (Cadson Bury)
A single Iron Age rampart and ditch circle the top of this steep hill overlooking the Lynher. It has two opposed and inturned entrances. These would have formed narrow defensible passages in front of the fort gates; with a wooden palisade on top, the ramparts presented a formidable obstacle. There are no traces of house platforms inside. The gap at the south is probably modern.

8 CAER BRAN
Hillfort
Walk View   SW 408290 (Caer Bran)
This well preserved Iron Age hillfort is reached by footpath from Carn Euny [G]. The inner rampart is very degraded whilst the outer rampart and ditch still present a formidable obstacle. In the centre is a round house. The site is bisected by the twin banks of a more modern track. There are traces of tinworks to the S and prehistoric/medieval field clearance mounds to the E and evidence of cultivation.

9 CARDINHAM
Church, Inscribed cross, Cross, Motte and bailey
[P]   SX 123687 (Church, Cardinham Castle)

Two crosses, formerly built into the east wall of the chancel, stand in the churchyard. Both are the best examples of their type in Cornwall. The smaller, a wheel-headed cross with projections, was originally a gravestone. The larger, a cross and ring with four holes at the angles of the cross arms, sits on a shortened shaft which has superb ornamentation. An inscription which appears to say ARTHI + is incomplete and would have given the name(s) of whoever was being commemorated. The church is largely unspoilt, 15th century in date with a Norman font, and 1401 brass. The powerful medieval family, the Cardinhams, had their castle here (a substantial motte and bailey of the 11th or 12th centuries), 700m to the SE near Old Cardinham Castle Farm (public access by permission only). Other family castles included Week St Mary [G] and Penhallam [G]. At Welltown (SX 136678) 1 1/4 miles SE of the church is another inscribed stone. 5th-6th century in date, it was for years

Decorated Cross, Cardinham churchyard

used as a gatepost. It says VAILATHI FILI VROCHANI which means 'The name (or monument or body) of Vailathus the son of Urochanus'.

10 CARN BREA
Neolithic enclosures, Round houses, Castle, Monument
[P] View   SW 685408 (Fort)

The hill has a long history. Most prominent today is the monument on the summit erected in 1836 by public subscription to the memory of Francis Basset of Tehidy whose family owed its enormous wealth to the mining industry. Much of the southern flanks of the hill are pock-marked with shafts and pits. The Bassets were an ancient local family; their small medieval castle (or perhaps a hunting lodge) stands on the eastern summit. First recorded in the 15th century it has seen various alterations in the 18th, 19th and 20th centuries and is now a restaurant.

Between the central and eastern summits may be seen several Iron Age hut circles, set in a huge 46 acre hillfort, the largest in Cornwall. The defences comprise two widely spaced ramparts enclosing the hill, and two smaller enclosures around the central and eastern summits. Excavations on the east summit have shown that the rampart is some 3,000 years older than the Iron Age. Traces of wooden buildings and Neolithic pottery were found behind the rampart, and the huge number of flint arrowheads (over 700) suggested that the site had been under attack. Much or all of the defences are likely to belong to the Neolithic rather than the Iron Age.

11 CARN GLUZE (BALLOWALL)
Chambered cairn
EH [P] View   SW 355312 (Chambered Cairn)

The barrow was discovered by the antiquarian Borlase in the 1870s; it had been buried beneath mine waste for many decades. The site is complex, having been rebuilt.
The sequence is likely to be :
1. Entrance Grave (on seaward side) within a 6-8m diameter kerbed cairn.
2. A small cairn built on the landward side

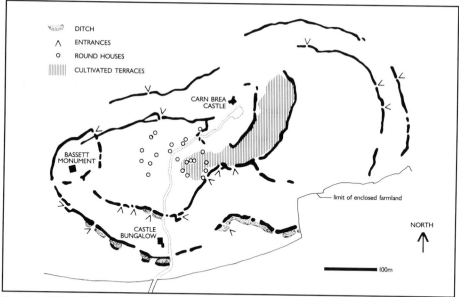

Carn Brea hillfort, Illogan, to the west of Redruth

containing several cists.

3. One cist built into the back of the Entrance Grave and another against the outer edge of the cairn. Then the whole covered by a massive cairn.

4. The outer of the inner walls built in the 1870s to enable the centre to be viewed.

It is late Neolithic-Early Bronze Age in date.

Carn Euny fogou

12 CARN EUNY
Courtyard house village, Fogou

EH [P] GD   SW 403288 (Settlement)

A hamlet of the Iron Age and Romano-British period (5th cent BC — 4th cent AD). It appears more haphazard in layout than Chysauster [G] and consists of at least 3 interlocking courtyard houses and several other stone round houses. Earlier wooden houses were replaced by stone and in its last phase (2-4th cent AD) by the courtyard houses. Within the settlement is a beautifully preserved Fogou (Halligye [G]).

13 CARNE (VERYAN) BEACON
Barrow

NT Walk Foot View [P]   SW 913387 (Tumulus)

The largest Bronze Age burial mound in Cornwall. Excavations in 1855 revealed a central stone cairn with a stone burial box (cist) containing a cremation. Other cremations were found close by. No evidence found to support the local story that King Gereint of Dingerein Castle (Hillfort across the other side of Gerrans Bay) was buried here in a golden boat with silver oars! 500m to the NW, and viewed from the road from Veryan to Pendower Beach, is Veryan Castle a fortified prehistoric farmstead.

Castle Dore hillfort, Fowey

14 CASTLE DORE
Hillfort

Walk   SX 103548

Well-preserved hillfort consisting of two substantial ramparts with the outer one curving out to enclose the entrance. 19th century visitors noted further outworks beyond the entrance. Excavations in 1936-7 confirmed that the ramparts were strengthened in the 1st century BC and there were many round houses in the interior and close to the entrance. The fortification may have seen action as a temporary refuge during the Civil War battle of Lostwithiel, 1644.

15 CASTLE AN DINAS, St Columb
Hillfort

CHT Walk View   SW 945623 (Fort)

One of the largest and best preserved Iron Age hillforts in Cornwall. Like Warbstow [G] a now degraded rampart inside the outer one is the 1st phase enclosure with a main entrance in the SE and five others around the circumference. This was abandoned and slighted and three massive ramparts built with an entrance in the SW. Other entrances are modern. There is a spring in the N sector and a mutilated Bronze Age burial mound lies in the S of the interior, a reminder that 500-1000 years earlier, hilltops were often used for burial.

A Wolfram mine (Tungsten) was opened here in the last war and an aerial ropeway traversed the site until the mid 1950s.

16 CHUN CASTLE
Hillfort, Chamber Tomb, Strip fields

Walk Foot View [P]

SW 405339 (Chun Castle, Chun Quoit)

An impressive double-walled stone built hillfort. In the 18th century the inner rampart was 15' high but in the 19th century the stone was used to build in Penzance (eg: Madron Workhouse). Main occupation was Iron Age (3rd-1st cent BC) with reoccupation in the Roman and Post-Roman period. Inside are a series of radiating enclosures with houses against the rampart. It is not possible to date these, nor the well. Hundreds of acres of prehistoric fields with their round houses and courtyard houses lie fossilised in the present field pattern on the slopes below the hillfort.

Chun Quoit 300m to W (SW 402400) is a Neolithic chamber tomb of the 4th millennium BC. The box-like structure with the enormous capstone originally stood on a wide stone platform. Adjacent on the S are the remains of prehistoric fields that appear to use the Quoit as a marker. These fields are partially overlain by medieval strip fields perhaps associated with Boswen, Keigwin or Bojewyan farms.

Castle-an-Dinas hillfort, St Columb Major

17 CHYSAUSTER
Courtyard house village
EH [P] Walk Foot GD SW 473350 (Settlement)
The best preserved and displayed example of
a courtyard house hamlet (for other see Carn
Euny [G]). It lies I mile E of Castle-an-Dinas
hillfort and although there is much evidence of
earlier settlement on the site all the visible
remains and the surrounding field boundaries
are Romano-British in date (2nd-4th cent AD).

18 ST CLEER HOLY WELL
Chapel and Cross
[P] SX 249683 (St Cleer's Well)
A beautiful granite baptistry, well and cross.
The 15th century building was restored in 1864.
It is square with a steep pitched roof and
pointed barrel vault. Arches around the front
and sides open into the building. Originally
there was an 8-10' square reservoir in front of
the building and a second basin inside. The
water flowed out under the E wall into a
bowssening (total immersion) pool used to
cure (? treat) the insane.
Bowssening consisted of being
pushed into the pool by a blow to
the chest, being tossed up and
down in the water until the
witless unfortunate was exhausted.
If sanity had not returned, following masses said in the church,
then bowssening commenced
again and again.. The cross has, on
both sides, two crosses in relief,
one within another.

19 ST CLEMENT
Inscribed stone
[P] GD SW 851439 (Church)
In the churchyard is a tall inscribed
stone (*right*) of AD 500-550 that
was remodelled as a cross in the
8th century. The inscription,
IGNIOC....VITALI FILI TORRICI
reads 'Ignioc...Vitalus son of Torri-
cus'. IGNIOC is a later addition
and only the second part is repeated in
Ogham though this has almost totally worn
away. Perhaps the later inscription and the
cross head were carved at the same time.

20 CONSTANTINE
Chapel and Holywell
Walk Foot SW 865749 (St Constantine' Church)
The chapel was semi-parochial (almost a parish
church) within St Merryn parish; larger and
more ornate than most Cornish chapels having
a small tower at the W end, a chancel, nave
and S aisle. Largely rebuilt in the 15th century;
cut stonework made of local cataclews stone
(quarry between Mother Ivey's and Harlyn
Bay). A graveyard and several houses were
known to surround it. Suppressed in c1540 it
became buried in sand until re-excavated in
1926. Close by is St Constantine's well, also
buried but excavated in 1911. The corbelled
slate well house had stone benches on either
side of a long cistern. Now consolidated and
covered with a modern shelter.

21 COTEHELE
House, Chapel
NT Walk [P] GD
SX 425685 (Cotehele Ho, Chapel)
The finest late medieval house in Cornwall.
The 15th and 16th century buildings are
grouped around a courtyard and approached
through a vaulted gatetower. The great hall is
adjoined by a late 15th century chapel. The
house was the principal residence of the
Edgcumbes until it was superseded by Mount
Edgcumbe in the late 16th century. In the
grounds is a small but well maintained chapel
commemorating the leap over the cliff to safety
of Sir Richard Edgcumbe in 1489. The
dovecote in the gardens is still inhabited!

Cotehele House, gatetower and front entrance.

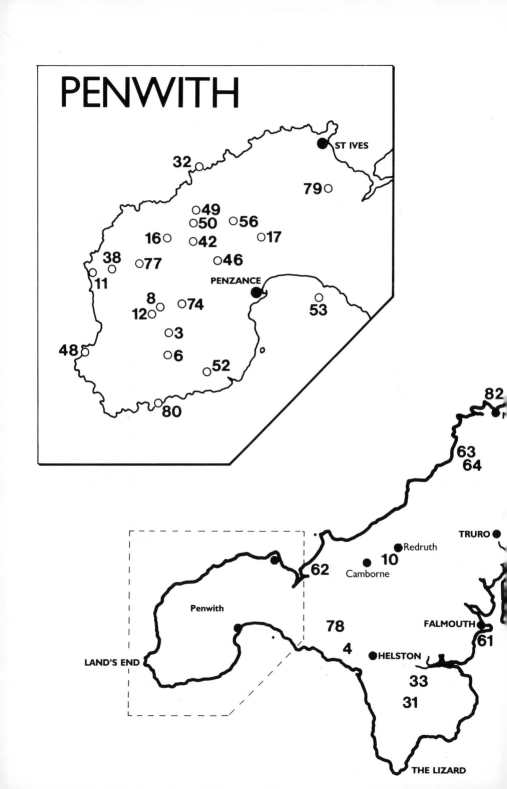

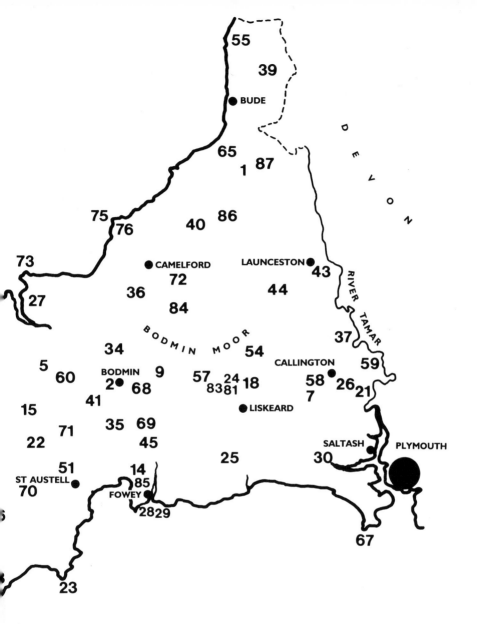

55

39

● BUDE

65

1 87

75
76

40 86

73

LAUNCESTON ●
43

● CAMELFORD

72

36

84

44

RIVER TAMAR

DEVON

27

BODMIN MOOR

54

37

34

CALLINGTON ●

59

5

60

BODMIN
2 ●

9

57 24 18
83 81

58 ●

26 21

7

68

41

● LISKEARD

15

22

71

35 69

45

25

SALTASH ●

30

PLYMOUTH ●

51

14
85

ST AUSTELL ●
70

FOWEY ●
28 29

67

23

CORNWALL

22 ST DENNIS
Hillfort, Church, Crosses
[P] View   SW 951583 (Church)
This hilltop church looks across Goss Moor to Castle-an-Dinas [G] hillfort. The name Dennis is derived from Dinas — fort. The churchyard wall, a massive construction, is part of the inner rampart of an Iron Age hillfort. Slight traces have been found of an outer rampart some 20m downhill. The church was gutted by fire in 1983. A cross stands near the S porch, the head is horseshoe shaped with a latin cross in outline, and on the shaft are unusual hour-glass designs.

23 THE DODMAN
Cliff castle
NT [P]-at Penare. Walk Foot SX 002395 (Fort)
The largest cliff castle (20 hectares) in the South West, it is defended by a single massive bank (The Bulwarks) and ditch. Inside are two Bronze Age burial mounds, the traces of a medieval strip field system, an early 19th century Watch house, and a memorial cross to a Royal Navy tragedy.

24 KING DONIERT'S STONE
EH [P]   SX 236688
A cross base found in a pit, near a cross shaft, was set up next to it in 1849. The cross base

has knot decoration of the 9th century and an inscription in Latin which reads DONIERT ROGAVIT PRO ANIMA which means 'Doniert has asked (prayers?) for (his?) soul'. Doniert is likely to be Dumgarth King of Cornwall who was drowned in AD 878. The cross shaft also has complex knotwork designs.

25 DULOE
Stone Circle
[P] Walk   SX 236583 (Stone circle)
Eight large quartz stones (one fallen). This, the smallest of Cornish circles, is just as likely to be the retaining kerb of a burial mound. An urn was found when a bisecting hedge was removed. Cairns with a similar kerb, with smaller stones, are found on Bodmin Moor.

26 DUPATH
Holy Well
EH Walk   SX 374693 (well)
This attractive granite building dates from 1510. An arched roof is topped with a bellcote-like turret over the entrance. It would have originally had an altar. The water was believed

King Doniert's Stone, St Cleer

Dupath Holy Well, near Callington

Duloe stone circle

to cure whooping cough and the basin is large enough to allow total immersion.

27 ST ENODOC
Church, Barrows
[P] — at Trebetherick or Rock. Walk Foot
SW 931773 (Church, Tumuli)

A small cruciform Norman church set at the head of a small, silted up, creek. Much of Norman date remains; 13th century tower and spire; 15th century south chancel chapel. Restored in 1873 having been only accessible for many years (due to sand dunes) via a hole in the roof. Sir John Betjeman is buried here. On Brea Hill, overlooking the church are three Bronze Age barrows. Between Brea Hill and Rock, are the buried remains of a Roman settlement (not visible), perhaps the Camel end of the routeway that follows the high ground via St Endellion, Tregeare Rounds, the milestones at Tintagel and Boscastle and on and up the north coast into Devon.

28 FOWEY
St Catherine's Castle
EH [P] — in Fowey. Walk Foot View SX 119509

An artillery fort built above Readymoney cove by Thomas Treffry of Place house in c1540; a small artillery fort similar to the water line forts at Pendennis [G] and St Mawes [G] it was designed to house several cannon, an officer and a few men. A late 19th and early 20th century quick-firing battery sits just below.

29 FOWEY
Fowey and Polruan blockhouses
[P] Walk SX 122513, 123511 (Blockhouses)

Built in 1457, in response to French raids, the blockhouses were part of a line of defences that included Dartmouth, Plymouth/Stone-house, and St Michael's Mount. A chain boom was stretched between the blockhouses, and

circular gun ports covered the entrance to the harbour. Five hundred years later, in the 2nd World War an anti-submarine boom was once again stretched between the blockhouses. The one on the Fowey side is ruinous and difficult to visit, that at Polruan has recently been restored and is easily accessible.

30 ST GERMANS CHURCH
Priory
[P] GD SX 359578

Built in the mid-12th century as a priory church it has the finest Norman west front to be seen in Cornwall or Devon and it is on the site of an important early monastery which in the 10th century was the seat of Cornish bishops. Continuing in use as a parish church the building survived the Reformation, though the choir was left to decay and collapse; only the nave and S aisle survives. Excavations earlier this century located the remains of a pre-Norman building beneath the chancel. North of the church, where the cloister stood, Port Eliot House (not open to the public) is built on the site of the monastic refectory, which it incorporates in its foundations.

The west front of St German's Church

31 GOONHILLY
Barrows and Standing Stone
[P] Walk GD **SW 726213** (Tumuli, Standing Stone)
Within the perimeter of Goonhilly Satellite Tracking Station are several large Bronze Age burial mounds. They are part of a large cemetery of barrows on Goonhilly Downs. Outside the fence is Dry Tree Menhir. The stone is gabbro from St Keverne parish, at least 2 miles distant and must have been a prominent landscape feature in the 2nd millennium BC.

32 GURNARD'S HEAD
Cliff Castle, Chapel
NT [P] – at Treen. Walk Foot
                    SW 432386 (Trereen Dinas, Chapel)
The narrow headland has 3 stone ramparts across its neck (the outer defence now only survives as a ditch). Up to 16 house platforms have been identified on the more sheltered E side, and were occupied in the Iron Age, with possible re-occupation in the Romano-British period. Immediately to the E along the coast was the 19th century site of a pilchard fishing station (seine) operated from a rough slipway and precarious wooden staging at the bottom of the cliff below Chapel Jane.
Chapel Jane (SW 434382 – AD 1100-1500) lies close to the edge of the cliff and is enclosed by an ill defined bank. The original chapel had a doorway in the centre of the S wall. At a later date this was blocked, an extension added to the W, and a door opened in the W wall. An altar stone (Mensa) in the west end has no consecration crosses on it showing that during mass a portable altar was placed on top as at Madron [G].

33 HALLIGYE FOGOU
Fogou
EH [P]   **SW 714239** (Fogou)
The Fogou is well-preserved and maintained. The farm in which it sits was the site of a settlement enclosure of the Iron Age and Romano-British period. The Fogou partly follows the line of the enclosure rampart, being dug underneath it, and one of the entrances (now blocked) opens out onto what would

have been the ditch. It seems likely that fogous were used for cold storage as well as acting as refuges in time of conflict.

34 HELLAND BRIDGE
[P]   SX 065715
It is a perfect looking bridge and one of the earliest (c1415) in the county; with four pointed arches and cutwaters. It replaced an earlier bridge here.

35 HELMAN TOR
Neolithic enclosure
[P] View   SX 062616
The rugged 2 acre hilltop is enclosed by a series of poorly defined, very ruinous ramparts. Part of the defensive circuit is formed by the vertical faces of the granite outcrops themselves. The rampart is clearest at the NE where excavation has shown it to have originally been a massive wall with traces of wooden structures behind, together with finds of flint arrowheads and pottery which date the site to the 4th millennium BC. The closest parallel in date, character and probably in function is Carn Brea [G]. Between the Tor and the road are the remains of a large prehistoric round house and associated field banks.

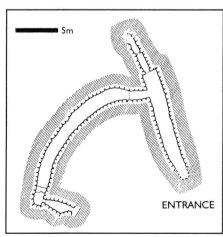

Halligye Fogou

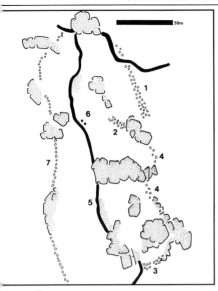

Helman Tor
I, 2, 3: Ramparts; 4: probable line of rampart;
5: modern hedge on line of rampart; 6: entrance?
7: outer work

36 HELSBURY BEACON
Hillfort and Chapel
[P] View   SX 083796 (Helsbury Castle)
A well-preserved Iron Age hillfort — an
enclosure surrounded by a single rampart and
ditch with an annexe attached at the entrance.
A holloway is traceable from the entrance,
running down towards the R. Camel. Part of
the annexe has been damaged by ploughing
and the rampart is cut by small quarries. In the
centre is a rectangular enclosure within which
are the remains of a chapel dedicated to
St Michael or St Syth.

37 HORSEBRIDGE
[P]   SX 400748 (Horsebridge)
Originally (built 1437) the link between Tavistock and Liskeard until Gunnislake New Bridge
[G] was built, it has six large round arches, a
wide flood water arch, and causeway on the
W side. The cutwaters and passing places are
large; there are stone brackets projecting from
near the top of the angles of the up-stream
cutwaters. The grooves/notches cut on the
underside seem to be for holding wooden
poles. They may be part of a salmon weir or

stake net connected with the Tavistock Abbey
fishery. See also Greystone Bridge SX 368804.

38 ST JUST IN PENWITH
Church, Inscribed stone, Cross,
Plain an Gwarry
[P] GD   SW 372315 (Church)
A 5th-6th century Inscribed stone attests the
early foundation of the site, as at Sancreed [G].
The stone has the inscription SENILUS IC
IACIT ('Senilus lies here') in Latin and on
another face an early form of cross, a Chi Rho.
Originally the church was called Lanuste,
containing the element Lann (enclosed Christian cemetery) although the circular plan has all
but disappeared. In the 9th/10th century the
carving of a fine interlaced cross was begun but
never completed. The unfinished shaft now
acts as a lintel over a recess in the N aisle. Its
closest parallel is the shaft at St Neot [G] and
King Doniert's stone [G]. Two small round
headed latin crosses are in the vicarage garden.
The church is mostly 15th century, the earlier
cruciform plan now largely gone. Unusually the
arcades are of Beer stone (Devon); the quality
of the carving is better than if they were
granite. Restoration in 1866 revealed six 15th
century wall paintings. Only two survive; those
of Christ of the Trades and George and the
Dragon.
Across the square from the church is St Just
Plain an Gwarry. This was an arena for
performing medieval Cornish miracle plays.
Like the Methodist preaching pits of the 18th
and 19th century, it consisted of tiered seating
or steps around a circular performance area.
The six stone steps noted by Borlase in 1769
have been replaced by a grassy bank.

39 KILKHAMPTON
Castle, Church and Medieval town
[P] GD   SS 253113 (Motte & Bailey)
Kilkhampton Castle (SS 243116) is a superbly
situated earthwork castle with a motte and two
baileys. Although it does not appear in
medieval documents it may well be an
'adulterine' (illegal) castle of the 12th century
civil war period, built either by the powerful
Earl Robert of Gloucester or more probably a

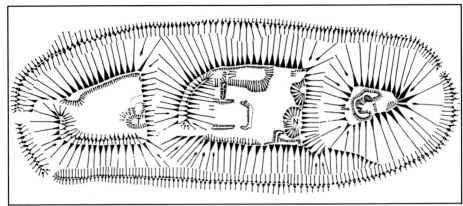

Kilkhampton, motte and bailey castle

local family, the Grenvilles. A low cross bank in the pasture field on the approach to the castle may be an outer defence, or even the rampart of an earlier promontory fort. In the innermost of the two baileys may be seen the slight foundations of at least 2 buildings, perhaps a hall and kitchen. On the top of the motte are traces of a possible tower. The banks surrounding the baileys would have been surmounted by wooden palisades.

In the 13th and 14th centuries Kilkhampton was a minor borough with a weekly market and three annual fairs. The triangular market place, centering on the churchyard, is now mostly infilled with houses. St James is a fine 16th century church with an excellent Norman south door.

40 LAMLAVERY
Deserted Medieval hamlet
[P] Walk　　　　　　　　　　SX 159834

One of the most complete examples of its kind, Lamlavery is set on a bleak and remote part of Davidstow Moor. It is mentioned in a document of 1440. The walls of houses and enclosures survive as turf-covered banks, forming a hamlet of five long-houses. Three or four have smaller outhouses or barns near them and all are associated with small enclosures (gardens, yards and rick stands). The long-houses are all aligned downslope; the lower end would have housed the animals. Slight but extensive traces of cultivation surround the settlement, probably for the growing of oats and rye.

41 LANIVET
Church, Crosses, Grave slabs, Inscribed stone
[P]　　　　　　　　　　SX 039642
　　　　　　　　　　　　(Church)

The church is mostly 15th century with no traces of earlier work; pre-conquest church site as evidenced by the Lann name and the circular churchyard. There is an Inscribed stone of the 5th-6th century in the church. It has a single name ANNICUS set within an incised border. There are two crosses and a coped stone in the church-yard: the first is the finest decorated wheel cross in Cornwall; the second is one of the finest decorated four-holed crosses; the 10th-11th century coped stone is one of only four in Cornwall and has a ridged and hipped top and is elaborately decorated.

42 LANYON QUOIT
Chamber tomb
NT [P]   SW 430337

A large capstone is supported by three uprights set in a very low long mound. The original plan is uncertain; it collapsed in 1815 and was re-erected in 1824 after public subscription. The chamber was originally a rectangular box set within a low long stone platform. At the other end are the remains of what were probably side chambers or cists.

43 LAUNCESTON
Town, Castle, Church, Priory, Bridge
EH [P] GD

Arguably the most important of Cornwall's medieval towns, Launceston (or Dunheved) was established by Robert of Mortain in the IIth century when he transferred the market at St Stephens to his new castle. It is the ancient town and monastery at St Stephens (lann + stefan + tun) which has given its name to Launceston. Launceston (Dunheved) is the only Cornish town to have had a town wall; the only remaining town gate is the 14th century South Gate, at one time used as the town prison. The church (St Mary Magdalene) is remarkable for its profusely ornamented exterior, built by Sir Henry Trecarrel in 1511-24. Dominating the town the castle was Cornwall's chief administrative centre for many centuries. The motte is crowned by a 12th century shell keep within which a round tower was built by Earl Richard in the 13th century. The bailey, with its N and S gates, contained a series of buildings including the 13th century Assize Hall, which continued in use to the 17th century; its excavated foundations are exposed. The castle was the site of the county gaol, notorious until its removal to Bodmin in 1835. At the foot of the hill to the N of the town St Thomas' Priory was one of the main religious houses in Cornwall, along with Bodmin [G] and St Germans [G]. Founded in 1127 by the Augustinians it replaced the older pre-norman monastery at St Stephens, it was dissolved 1536-39; the buildings were used briefly as stables, bakehouses and piggeries before

demolition in the same century; much of the stone was used to build in Launceston, the entrance to the White Hart Hotel being a fine example. The site was rediscovered in the late 19th century during the construction of the L&SWR line and the town Gasworks. The layout is typical: a range of buildings surrounding a cloister — on N the Priory church; W the Prior's lodgings and kitchens; S the lavatory, cellars and refectory; E the Day room, dormitory, chapter house and sacristy. Only the central part of the church with its N and S aisles and nave are visible as ruins between the Church and the Launceston Steam Railway site. Much of the rest has been destroyed or still lies buried under nearby buildings.

Nearby is a delightful medieval pack horse bridge (SX 328852), with five small arches, with cutwaters but no parapets.

44 LEWANNICK CHURCH
Church, Inscribed stones
[P]   SX 276807 (Church)

The church is almost entirely 15th century apart from the Norman font and the 19th century S arcade. Its early origins are attested by two 5th-7th century inscribed stones. The stones have both Latin and Irish ogham script and on each the inscription is repeated in both languages. The stone in the church reads in

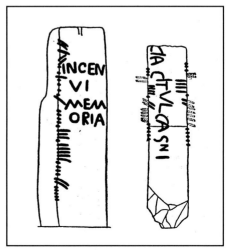

Inscribed stones, Lewannick

Latin: C IACIT VLCAGNI (Here lies Ulcagnus) and the Ogham which is repeated on both front edges reads ULCAGNI. The stone in the churchyard reads in Latin INCENVI MEMORIA, and the Ogham on the front left edge IGENAVI MEMOR. This translates as 'The memorial of Igenavus'. The name of Lewannick means the 'lann of Wenoc' and the circular embanked churchyard preserves the form of the early enclosure.

45 LOSTWITHIEL
Duchy Palace, Town, Church, Bridge
[P] GD   SX 107598
Built by Earl Edmund in 1289 the once impressive complex of the 'Duchy Palace' was never a residence but an administrative centre serving four main purposes: the management of the Cornish Duchy estates; the venue for the County Court and for the election of the Knights of the Shire; the 'palace' served as Coinage Hall for the assaying of tin; it housed the Stannary prison. A print of 1734 shows the ruins of a massive hall, the shell of which still survives incorporated into shops and houses. There is an arched passageway at the W end, and truncated buttresses can still be seen at the front. Part of the front wall was removed to

insert an 18th century prison (note the barred upper windows). Immediately to the E of the hall is a better preserved part of the complex, now the Masonic Hall; this may have been the tinners' Convocation Hall.

Lostwithiel, with a charter dated to 1189, was an important port until shipping was blocked by the silting of the Fowey. The town is unusual in Cornwall, in being planned. It still retains its grid iron pattern of streets. The Bridge is at the lowest crossing point of the Fowey and marks the upper limit of the medieval wharfs; built in 1437, it has 5 pointed arches with cut waters and passing places. The parapet was added in 1676. By 1539 tin streaming on Bodmin Moor caused tin waste to nearly choke the arches and the river channel. A new channel to the E was dug with a wooden bridge built over it. This was rebuilt in stone in the 18th century. On the W side was a long arched causeway; this now lies beneath West Street. Like Wadebridge and the old Looe bridge a chapel was built at one end. None of these now survive.

The church has a fine spire and 13th century tower, and belongs mostly to the 14th century (unusual in Cornwall). There is a medieval

The Duchy Palace, Lostwithiel; a view from an engraving of 1734 by Samuel and Nathaniel Buck

lantern cross in the churchyard and the 13th century font is particularly decorative.

46 MADRON
Holy Well, Well-chapel
Walk Foot   SW 456333

The well is a small rectangular basin set at ground level from which the water flows NE 50 yards to the well-chapel. This very early site has always been a popular place of pilgrimage and visitors still tie votive rags to bushes. The water is reputed to cure rickets and assist in divination.

The chapel, in ruins for nearly 200 years has now been restored. In the right hand corner opposite the entrance is the font or place of baptism which can still be filled with water. The chapel lies inside a small, probably medieval, enclosure. The granite altar slab or mensa and the lower courses of the walls may date from the 12th century as do the seats and chancel division. The chapel and well are part of a complex that has claim to be the original location of St Madern's cult.

47 ST MAWES CASTLE
Castle
EH [P] GD View   SW 841327

Built at the same time as Pendennis [G], St Mawes is of different design. Consisting of a central tower with three bastions attached to it like a clover leaf. Both castles are beautifully built and despite their stern purpose, manage to combine a certain medieval elegance and romance. There was also an auxiliary fort at the waterline but only the lower walls survive. St Mawes never developed into a large garrison over the succeeding centuries, remaining instead a battery position.

48 MAYON (MAEN) CASTLE
Cliff Castle
NT Walk Foot View   SW 348257 (Maen Castle)

The cliff castle cuts off a small promontory with a ditch, (with an external bank), protecting an inner stone-built rampart. At c500BC it is one of the earliest cliff castles in Cornwall. Adjoining are the extensive and possibly contemporary remains of a prehistoric field system consisting of banks and slight cultivation scarps.

49 MEN SCRYFA
Inscribed Stone
[P] Walk   SW 467353

Perhaps originally a Bronze Age standing stone the 5th-7th debased Latin inscription reads RIALOBRANI CUNOVALI FILI – (the grave, memorial) of Rialobranus son of Cunovalus.

50 MEN AN TOL
Holed stone
Walk Foot

SW426349 (Men an Tol)

A holed stone with two uprights on either side: an enigmatic form of Bronze Age monument, probably now incomplete.

Men Scryfa

51 MENACUDDLE
Holy Well
[P]   SX 013535 (Well Chapel)

Standing in this beautiful wooded valley was an important medieval chapel. Only the adjacent 15th century holy well remains. The attractive granite well house has two arched entrances and a small window in the west wall. The east wall is built against the natural rock and the water springs from its base. The water was renowned for aiding divination, good fortune (throwing in bent pins) and the cure of ulcers.

52 MERRY MAIDENS AREA
Stone Circle, Standing Stones, Entrance Grave
EH [P] Walk Foot

SW 432245 (Stone Circle, Standing Stones)

The area contains an astonishing range of ritual and burial monuments. The Merry Maidens (SW 432 244) has carefully chosen and regularly spaced stones and is a perfect circle.

Until the 1860s there was another circle nearby. On the road verge close by are the remains of Tregiffian Entrance Grave (late Neolithic): kerbed cairn with a chamber, covered over with large roof slabs, built into the edge of the mound. Across the road in a hedge (SW 429244) is the Goon Rith standing stone. Along the road towards Newlyn are The Pipers standing stones. These two menhirs are the tallest still standing in Cornwall. They are reputedly the two pipers who lured the merry maidens to dance on a Sunday. All were turned to stone.

There are two medieval stone crosses on the road to the W.

53 ST MICHAEL'S MOUNT
Priory, Fortification
NT Walk (tidal)   SW 515299 (Priory)

The Mount's spectacular setting is matched by its long and fascinating past. Much can still be seen of the Benedictine Priory, which was established before the Norman Conquest. It was famous as a place of pilgrimage. The Priory Church, on the summit, is largely 14th century. The priory was closely associated with the town of Marazion, where it had a market from the 11th century. Both before and after the Reformation the Mount was garrisoned to defend the coast. Held by the Royalist Sir Francis Basset during the Civil War it was surrendered in 1646 and since 1647 has been the home of the St Aubyn family.

The Pipers standing stones

54 MINIONS AREA
Hillfort **SX 257726 (Stowe's Pound)** Walk View
Rillaton Barrow **SX 269719 (Tumulus)** Walk
Stone Circles **SX 258714 (The Hurlers)** EH Walk

Two stone enclosures encompass Stowe's Hill. A larger enclosure at the N end of the hill is attached to a smaller one that lies above the disused Cheesewring Quarry. The ramparts are of tumbled stone, and must originally have stood at least 2-3m high. The walls were

'The North East Prospect of St Michael's Mount in Cornwall', 1758   *Royal Institution of Cornwall*

probably of coursed stone with tall upright stones to the front and rear. Apart from several small gaps the main entrances are on the W and E and are flanked by antennae walls that double back to encompass the hill. Inside the large enclosure are two Bronze Age cairns and one stone round house. In addition there are over 100 house platforms, where stone has been cleared to one side to allow the erection of wooden houses. The design of the enclosure and the presence of these platforms suggests that like Roughtor [G] this is Bronze Age or Neolithic and is related to the settlements and ritual monuments in the vicinity.

○ HOUSE SITES

STOWE'S POUND

10m

DISUSED QUARRY

Close to Minions village are The Hurlers: three stone circles in a line. The S one is badly damaged and the other two have been partially excavated and restored. To the W are two standing stones, 'The Pipers'. They may be contemporary and associated with the circles. The circles lie in a 'sacred area' with another circle on Craddock Moor (SX 2486 7183 – all the stones are fallen) a Stone Row (SX 241721) and many burial cairns, on the surrounding hills. Bronze Age settlements and fields lie around the edges, particularly below

The Hurlers, stone circles

Tregarrick Tor and on Craddock Moor.

The Rillaton Barrow can be seen on the horizon beyond the circles. It is one of the largest burial mounds on the Moor. A large stone cist (burial box) was discovered in 1837 and contained the remains of an extended skeleton with a pot and other goods near the chest. The pot contained a ribbed cup of beaten gold. It was lost for many years but was 'rediscovered' in King George V's dressing room and contained his collar studs. There is a copy in Truro Museum. A few metres to the N are the low battered traces of a platform cairn. The cairns marked on the OS map on Tregarrick Tor, Craddock Moor and Caradon Hill show a great variety in shape and size. They are good examples of the range of burial sites on the Moor.

55 MORWENSTOW
Church, Holywell

[P] GD   SX 205153 (Church)

Norman church with N aisle and 15th century tower and S aisle. Fine Norman doorway with carvings of the heads of men and beasts; pre-Norman font; part of a wall painting of St Morwenna and many superb bench ends. Parson Hawker was vicar here for 40 years and his vicarage has chimneys based on two Oxford colleges, three church towers and his mother's gravestone. There are several churchyard memorials to shipwrecked sailors. In the old vicarage garden adjacent is the Holy well dedicated to St John the Baptist. First mentioned in 1296, the small corbelled well house is in good condition.

56 MULFRA QUOIT
Chamber Tomb

Walk Foot View   SW 451353

Similar to Chun Quoit [G]. The large capstone has slipped to one side, probably when the fourth sidestone was removed. The chamber sits within a low stone platform. There are several Bronze Age barrows along the ridge to the N. A low field bank joins the monument, being part of a prehistoric field system that stretches down the hill to the SW.

57 ST NEOT
Church, Churchyard Cross, Holywell

[P] Walk Foot GD   SX 187678 (Church, well)

Church restored in 19th century; 15th century three tier tower and impressive embattled south aisle and porch. Renowned for its

Lantern Cross, Mawgan-in-Pydar

15th/16th century stained glass: 15 windows have at least 50% original glass (restored in 1826); they tell the story of saints and angels, the Flood, and St Neot.

The shaft from a late 9th century cross is the best example of interlaced work on a granite cross in Cornwall (others similar at King Doniert's stone [G], Phillack [G], Lanivet [G], Sancreed [G], Cardinham [G]); re-erected in 1889 and placed on St Neot's stone outside the porch. Tradition says that St Neot was so small that he could not reach the church door keyhole; he used to stand on this stone and throw the key into the keyhole. The 3 latin crosses have been brought to the churchyard from elsewhere in the parish (wayside crosses), and the 15th century Lantern cross comes from St Kew.

There were many medieval tin works in the parish and it was consequently relatively wealthy. A mortar stone from a tin stamping mill bearing the impression of the stamps is set into a wall opposite the Post Office.

The holy well is 400m W of the church in a field on the N side of the river and is reached by a track. It is a small stone building with a door below ground level giving access to a bench seat at the rear. St Neot used to stand in the well immersed to his neck (or waist) reciting the Psalter.

58 NEWBRIDGE Callington

[P]   SX 348680 (Newbridge)
Built in c1470 this and the Newbridge at Gunnislake [G] provided a quicker journey from Tavistock to Liskeard via Callington. It replaced Horsebridge [G] several miles up river. The four round arches have massive piers with cut waters and passing places. Like Horsebridge the cut waters have stone brackets projecting near the top. The bridge was probably the lowest limit of the Rillaton Fishery (Duchy of Cornwall), so the brackets may have secured a stake net.

59 NEWBRIDGE Gunnislake

[P]   SX 433722 (New Br)
Until 1961 Newbridge was the lowest road crossing on the Tamar and linked Tavistock and Liskeard. Built c1510 it has 6 slightly pointed arches. The bridge was hotly contested in the Civil War when Lord Essex for Parliament took the bridge (20 dead) from Sir Richard Grenville for the King (200 dead and prisoners). A month later Essex was defeated at Lostwithiel.

60 NINE MAIDENS
Stone Row

[P] Walk Foot   SW 937676 (Nine Maidens)
The stone row now consists of 9 stones in line. A tenth stone between no 7 and 8 is a recent addition. The stump of a further stone on the same line, the 'Old Man' or 'Magi

Nine Maidens stone row, St Column Major

Stone' survives 500m to the NE. Early Bronze Age in date (c2,000 BC) it is assumed that this was a ritual or ceremonial monument. Seven others are known from Bodmin Moor and many others on Dartmoor.

61 PENDENNIS CASTLE

EH [P] GD View   *(see next page)*
                        SW 824318 (Pendennis Castle)
By 1530 Falmouth was the only major port in the south west not defended by artillery blockhouses and chain booms. Despite an attack on a Spanish Fleet by four French men-of-war in Falmouth haven in 1537 it was to be two years later after Spain and France together threatened England that Falmouth was fortified.

Pendennis guarded the western side and St Mawes [G] the eastern side of the Fal estuary. Pendennis (Pen-dinas: meaning fort) was built on the site of an Iron Age cliff castle. The new artillery fort consisted of three elements, built between 1540 and 1550; the central round tower with guns on the roof and two gundecks; around it a lower battery or terrace for fourteen guns; a separate entrance or lodgings block. At the tip of the headland an auxiliary fort (Little Dennis) provided powerful support at sea level. Pendennis developed as a complex fortress up until 1956 when it was decommissioned.

Pendennis Castle from the air

62 PHILLACK CHURCH
Inscribed stone, Grave slab, Cross

P] GD   SW 565385

Although the church was largely rebuilt in 1856-7 a wealth of evidence from the Early Christian period survives. In the porch gable is a small stone inscribed with a Chi-Rho symbol; this comprises the letters X and P, in Greek the first two letters of CHRISTOS. This is the earliest evidence for Christianity in Cornwall and dates to the 5th century. South-east of the church is a 7th century inscribed stone reading CLOTUALI MOBRATTI — '(The grave of) C, the son of M.'
In the church is a 9th century slab with an incised crucifix, and outside, between tower and porch, is a ridged 9th-11th century tomb cover or 'coped stone' see Lanivet [G]. The fine churchyard cross (S of the church) is probably of the 11th century. (Two later crosses may also be seen).

63 ST PIRAN'S ORATORY; ST PIRANS SECOND CHURCH
Cross

P] Walk Foot   SW 768564; SW 772565

There was an important early monastery here; Domesday Book records that the Canons of St Piran held 'Lanpiran'. It was one of the foremost places of pilgrimage in medieval Cornwall; the shrine contained the relics of St Piran and also teeth of St Brendan and St Martin. The small pre-Norman chapel or Oratory with its surrounding graveyard became overwhelmed by sand during the medieval period. Excavated in the 19th century, it had to be reburied in 1981 to secure the structure. The site is marked by a memorial stone. Four hundred metres to the east are the ruined walls of the old parish church, itself aban-

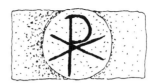

Chi-Rho stone, Phillack

doned to the sand in 1804. By the church is a fine cross (a useful landmark) which may well be one recorded as a boundary point in a charter of AD960. The outline of the old churchyard can still be traced, particularly on the S side where it is defined by a broad low bank. The large size of the churchyard suggests that it may be the original monastic enclosure of 'Lanpiran'.

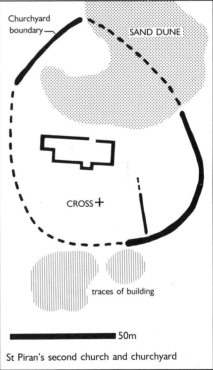

St Piran's second church and churchyard

64 ST PIRAN'S ROUND
Round and Plain an Gwarry

PC [P]   SW 779545 (St Piran's Round)

Originally an Iron Age/Romano-British enclosed farmstead it was converted in the medieval period to a Playing Place (Cornish: Plain an Gwarry). Miracle plays were performed here watched by the audience sitting around the inside of the amphitheatre. The depression in the middle (The Devil's Spoon) was the place where the Devil sprang from during the performances. Still used for meetings and entertainment. See St Just [G].

65 POUNDSTOCK
Church and Guildhouse
[P] GD   SX 202994 (Church)
An early church site dedicated to the Celtic Saint Winwaloe. Some of the stonework is early: N aisle, tower and porch 15th century; font 13th century; Medieval wall paintings. Adjacent to the Church is a two storey 15th century guildhouse with stone buttresses and wooden mullioned windows. This beautiful and well-maintained building was probably built for the medieval equivalent of a Friendly Society for the mutual benefit of parishioners. The Church has seen great controversy — a rector excommunicated in 1261; a rector re-installed by the Archbishop of Canterbury himself at Poundstock in 1282; a curate murdered by parishioners in the chancel in 1357.

Probus Church

66 PROBUS
Church
[P] GD   SW 899478 (Church)
A pre-Norman monastic foundation, it later became a collegiate church with a dean and five canons. Although it was a Norman church it is now largely a 15th century building. The tower is the tallest in Cornwall and is both elaborate and beautiful.

Restormel Castle, Lostwithiel

Resugga hillfort

67 RAME HEAD
Cliff Castle, Chapel

[P] – at Coastguard Station. Walk Foot View

SX 418483 (Fort, Chap)

The headland was defended in the Iron Age by a deep rock-cut ditch crossing the neck. There are only slight traces of a rampart on the inner side. Several round house platforms stand on the slope behind, although wartime fortifications have disturbed the area to the E of the footpath. Licensed in 1397, the chapel, standing on the highest point, has a vaulted granite roof, and a stairway to a bell turret. Some windows are blocked and the tracery of the chancel window has gone. It also served as a lighthouse and watchhouse (a watchman was employed at the time of the Armada). Wartime installations lie adjacent.

68 RESPRYNN BRIDGE

[P]

SX 099636

On the old road from Bodmin to Looe. There was a ford (Res) and a chapel of St Martin here by the 12th century and a bridge by 1300. Built in c1520 it has 5 arches of different sizes and dates: the middle one is smallest, oldest and slightly pointed; others are rounded and the two on the west are modern. There are

cutwaters and passing places. Set just below Lanhydrock Park it was of great strategic significance in the Civil War battle of Lostwithiel, 1644.

69 RESTORMEL CASTLE

EH [P] Walk GD

SX 104614 (Castle)

The impressive 12th century shell keep is built into the inner face of an earlier ring-work. Ranges of buildings built against the shell keep would originally have been of timber; in the 13th century these were rebuilt in stone by Earl Richard or his son Earl Edmund. The castle was twice visited by the Black Prince, and saw brief action in the Civil War. The castle is approached through the site of the bailey; slight platforms for buildings (such as hall and stables) may still be seen.

70 RESUGGA CASTLE
Hillfort

[P] Walk View

SW 940511 (Resugga Castle)

Sets on the edge of a spur overlooking the confluence of the St Stephen and Fal rivers, it consists of a D-shaped enclosure with an outwork, or annexe attached to the N side. A well pronounced holloway leads from the road through the centre of the annexe into the enclosure. It is a typically strongly defended hillfort of the Iron Age.

71 ROCHE ROCK
Chapel

[P] Walk   SW 991596 (Chap)

The chapel to St Michael was built in 1409 on the top of a remarkable granite Tor and is one of the best known landmarks in Cornwall. It consists of a lower chamber (Priest's room) that uses the natural rock for the N and W walls. Above is the chapel. Some cut stone-work survives.

Roche Rock Chapel

72 THE ROUGHTOR AREA
Hillfort, prehistoric houses, fields and burial cairns, Chapel

NT (Roughtor) [P] Walk Foot View

SX 147808 (Settlement, Cairns, Stone circle)

Looking across to Roughtor from the car park the slopes are covered with Bronze Age field walls, the ruins of c100 round houses and burial cairns. This area is one of the most accessible and visible areas of prehistoric

landscape in Britain. There are in the area 3 stone circles, over 250 round houses, 60 cairns, many hectares of field systems, and a deserted medieval farm.

Walk to the N of Roughtor to Showery Tor, passing through prehistoric fields and a cairn cemetery. It is a spectacular pile of natural stones around which a ring cairn is built. Walk S along the ridge to Little Rough Tor (another large cairn). Between here and Roughtor are several stone ramparts encompassing both sides of the hill top — there are traces of round house platforms inside the hillfort. There are two entrances on the sides facing the car park and Brown Willy. Both have small kerbed cairns at the entrances suggesting an Early Bronze Age or even Neolithic date for the enclosure (see Stowes Pound [G]). On top of Roughtor are the remains of the Chapel of St Michael. Set within the mutilated remains of a Bronze Age cairn the walls are now only just discernible. Licensed in 1371, it acted as a guide to travellers on the Moor. To the E are steps leading down the steep Tor edge to a rectangular building perhaps where the priest lived. During the period of its use there were medieval farms at Fernacre, Brown Willy, Garrow Tor, Louden Hill [G], Stannon and at Lamlavery [G] on Davidstow Moor, amounting to perhaps 20-30 or more households. There is a well, perhaps a holy well, on the N slopes below Little Rough Tor.

Scramble to the S end of the Tor and look S to Fernacre Stone Circle below. To the SW below Louden Tor are two ruined rectangular buildings — the medieval farm of Louden. The whole of the hill was enclosed by a bank, and the slopes facing Roughtor cultivated.

73 THE RUMPS
Cliff castle

NT [P] Walk View   SW 934811 (Fort)

One of the most spectacular sites in the county. Excavated in 1963-67, the site was occupied between 4th century BC and 1st cen AD. Round houses were found with pottery, bones and other artefacts suggesting a settled occupation much the same as in inland hillforts

The Rumps, Iron Age cliff castle

eg: Warbstow [G]). Traces of hut platforms can be seen behind the inner rampart and on the slopes of the E knoll, along with the lines of at least two fields. The ramparts (numbered 1-4 outwards) are part of two phases. In Phase 1 ramparts 1 (inner) and 3 were built with a large area, perhaps of defended grazing, between them.

Phase 2 — Ramparts 2 and 4 (outer) built, Rampart 1 still in use, Rampart 3 abandoned. A modern wall has been built into the outer rampart. The defences were at their most complex, with massive wooden gateways and walkways over the top, just before abandonment.

74 SANCREED
Church, Crosses, Well & Chapel
[P]   SX 420293 (Church)

There are two notable crosses in the church-yard. The first is 10th century and has the maker's name RUNHO carved on the front. A cross now at Lanherne, St Mawgan SW 872659 but originally from Roseworthy, W of Camborne is by the same hand (RUHOL). The cross head from St Buryan [G] appears to be of similar design and it is thought that a

western style developed perhaps associated with the 10th century charter of King Athelstan to St Buryan church. The second was originally an inscribed stone probably reading EROCAV....FILIUS IC.... The inscription has been worn away but it would have read: Erocav (the father) his son lies here.... — the son's name included here. In the 13th century the stone was turned upside down and carved to look like the first cross. The gothic vase and fleur de lys incised design are of this date.

The inscribed stone and the characteristically circular shape of the churchyard suggest an early foundation. The church is largely 13th-15th century and part of the decorated chancel screen is preserved.

In and on the church yard wall are two other wheel-headed crosses, brought from farms in the 19th century where they served as wayside markers. 300m to the west are the ruins of a chapel and holy well in a modern enclosure.

Crosses in Sancreed churchyard

75 TINTAGEL CASTLE

EH [P] View GD   SX 050892 (Castle)

The spectacular setting of the castle is such that we should not be surprised to find it a magnet for Arthurian myth and legend. This should not be allowed to obscure the importance of its actual history.

The most obvious remains on the headland are those of the 13th century castle built by the colourful Earl Richard. More important to the archaeologist are the very slight traces of over 70 enigmatic rectangular buildings. Excavations in the 1930s produced huge quantities of 6th century wares imported from the Mediterranean, more than is known from any other site in Britain. Twelfth century literature, derived from Cornish folklore, depicts Tintagel as the seat of Cornish rulers, King Mark in the celebrated romance of Tristan and Isolt, Duke Gorlois in Geoffrey of Monmouth's History of the Kings of Britain. The folklore traditions, combined with the archaeological evidence, suggests that Tintagel was a royal seat of the 6th century. It may well have been the importance of these traditions that led Earl Richard to build his castle on this strategically

remote headland. It became disused in the 14th century.

76 TINTAGEL
Church, Burial mounds, Earthwork, Roman milestone

[P] View GD   SX 051885 (Church)

A Norman or earlier cruciform church with many early details remaining. The Roman milestone (AD250) was found in 1889 acting as a lych stone at the SE churchyard entrance. It reads (I)MP C G VAL LICIN (to the Emperor Caesar Gaius Valerius Licinius). There is another stone (AD251-3) at Trethevy 1.5 miles to the NE.

The churchyard itself is complex and ancient. Burials found in the field to the N suggest that it was originally larger, and an earthwork which may be seen immediately to the NW may be part of the original extent. Within the earthwork and churchyard are a series of mounds conceivably a dynastic cemetery associated with the 5th-6th century royal stronghold of Tintagel headland.

77 TREGESEAL CIRCLES
(THE DANCING STONES, THE NINE MAIDENS)

Walk Foot   SW 386324 (Stone circle)

This area can be approached via the Tinners Track footpath along Kenython Lane from the W or from the B3318 to the NE. Originally two circles, that surviving lies in moorland and has been restored. Within this 'sacred area' are a number of large burial mounds and the Kenidjack Holed Stones. Similar in concept though smaller than Men an Tol [G] and The Tolvan (SW 706 283), they consist of five stones with hour glass shaped holes through their centres (600m NNE of the stone circle). A number of prehistoric settlements exist in the area.

78 TREGONNING HILL
Hillfort, 2 Rounds, Medieval Fields

[P]—at Balwest Chapel. Walk Foot View
          SW 599300 (Castle Pencaire, Round, Round)

At the E end of the hill is the former site of an Armada Beacon and remains of several cairns lie along the spine. At the W end is Castle

Tregonning Hill from the north

Pencaire, a hillfort with two stone ramparts, now badly quarried away and with a war memorial standing on the inner rampart. As well as mining pits there are several circular house platforms in the interior. In the field below and to the NE are two enclosed farms (rounds) of the Iron Age or Romano British period. The E one is the best preserved in Cornwall, with an entrance track and traces of round houses along the inside of the rampart. There are clear traces of strip fields defined by low banks between the three monuments. These are clear evidence of later medieval cultivation, probably associated with Tregonning Farm.

79 TRENCROM CASTLE
Hillfort
NT [P] Walk Foot View   SW 518362 (Fort)
A fabulous view over St Ives Bay and St Michael's Mount. An Iron Age hillfort with a

single stone rampart made up in places of stones on edge, back and front; two entrances on E and W side, each with two large gateposts in the interior. There are a number of round houses some of which have been disturbed by quarrying. The track entering from the N is a quarry track.

80 TRERYN DINAS
Cliff castle   (see plan on next page)
[P] — in Treen village. NT Walk Foot View
                    SW 397221 (Treryn Dinas)
Sited on one of the most spectacular stretches of coast, the Iron Age cliff castle is both large and complex. Four massive ramparts and ditches enclose the whole headland. The craggy end of the headland is cut off by a single bank and ditch with two house platforms visible on each side of the entrance.

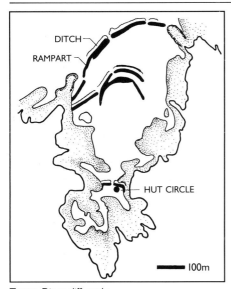

Treryn Dinas cliff castle

Trethevy Quoit

81 TRETHEVY QUOIT
Chamber Tomb
EH [P]   SX 259688 (Trethevy Quoit)
Impressive Neolithic (c3,500BC) tomb consisting of 6 large side stones, supporting a massive capstone. At the highest end one of originally two stones acts as a pillar of a forecourt. The structure originally stood on a wide stone platform, the remains of which can still be seen. Whilst access to the inside was by a small rectangular hole in the front, the small hole in the capstone remains unexplained. Its burial function is unclear although it must have acted as a territorial focus along with another one at Bearah Common on Bodmin Moor

(SX 263744 — on N side of track leading t Bearah Quarry).

82 TREVELGUE HEAD
Cliff Castle, Barrows
[P] — at Porth. LA Walk View
                SW 82516304 (Fort, Tumul
The headland is cut off by a series of ramparts and is the most heavily defende prehistoric site in Cornwall. The seaward h of the site is now an island joined by a bridg the original entrance was approximately whe the cliff is on the Porth beach side. On th island are traces of field banks and hous platforms. Excavations show a long b interrupted occupation from at least the 3 century BC to the 6th century AD as well evidence for bronze and iron smelting. The are two Bronze Age barrows here, one on th island and the other on the North cliff.

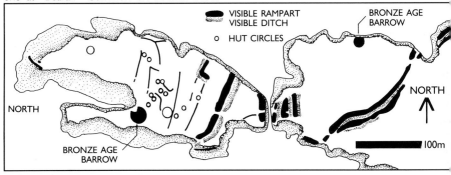

Trevelgue cliff castle, Newquay

Treverbyn Bridge, St Neot

83 TREVERBYN BRIDGE

[P]   SX 206675

On the old road from Liskeard to St Neot and Bodmin. This most attractive bridge was rebuilt in 1412-13. The larger part of the bridge has two pointed arches with cutwaters and passing places and the other earlier section over the tributary has one arch. See also Pantersbridge X 159680.

84 TRIPPET STONES
Stone Circle

[P] Walk   SX 131750 (Stone Circle)

This is a most attractive circle. Truly circular, it consists of a ring of large stones of which almost half are now missing. Near the centre is a modern boundary stone.

85 TRISTAN STONE
or THE LONGSTONE
Inscribed stone

[P]   SX 112522 (Long Stone)

The inscription reads CIRVSINIVS (or CIRCSIUS or DRUSTANVS) HIC IACIT CVNOMORI FILI—Cirusinius (or Cirusius or Drustanus) lies here, son of Cunomorus. 6th century in date the stone has been linked to the Tristan and King Mark legend. There is a tau or 'T' shaped cross on the back at the top.

86 WARBSTOW BURY
Hillfort

LA [P] View   SX 202908 (Warbstow Bury)

One of the largest Iron Age hillforts in Cornwall. Like Castle-an-Dinas [G] and The Rumps [G] it shows evidence of a change in layout. The defences consist of two massive ramparts and ditches and between them the degraded remains of a third (Phase I enclosure). In the last few centuries BC it was replaced and slighted. The later, very large, ramparts have traces of banks on the outside edges of their ditches. These are counterscarp banks caused by dumping material dug out of the ditches during their maintenance. The two original entrances are inturned and opposite each other on the NW and SE sides. It is likely that many round houses were built within the inner enclosure of this important chieftain's stronghold. A long mound in the middle known as the Giant's Grave is probably a medieval rabbit warren.

87 WEEK ST MARY
Church, Medieval Town, Castle and Grammar school

[P] GD   SX 237977 (Earthwork)

Now a quiet village, Week St Mary was established as a small borough in the 13th century, with a weekly market and twice yearly

Week St Mary

fairs. The medieval layout of burgage plots (strip gardens of the town Burgesses) may still be seen, and in particular the site of a very large triangular market place around the church, now largely infilled with houses.

The church is mostly 14th-15th century with a three stage tower and porch with room over (parvise). On the footpath just W of the churchyard is the castle mound. Though small and weak compared to most mottes, its rim is likely to have supported a palisade, and in the centre would have been a tower or building. Surrounding the mound are earthworks of enclosures and building platforms associated with the castle. It was probably built by Richard Fitzturòld tenant of the Conqueror's half brother Robert of Mortain. In the 12th and 13th centuries it belonged to the de Wics, who also held land on Scilly. The town was established either by the de Wics or by their successors,

the Blanchminsters. To the E of the churchyard is Week St Mary Grammar School, which can be viewed from the road. Founded in 1508 by Dame Thomasine Percival the principal remains are a battlemented wall and a 16th century house with carved tympanum over the front door and at the back a stair turret, massive lateral chimney stack, and round headed mullioned windows. In 1546 the school was described as 'a great comfort to all in the country' who sent their children to board there, but in 1548, perhaps as a result of local politics, it was moved to Launceston.

88 YEOLM BRIDGE

[P]   SX 318873 (Yeolmbridge)

Oldest and best finished bridge in Cornwall two pointed arches with supporting ribs of 14th century date. The chamfered ribs bear a close resemblance to the arch of the N gate of Launceston Castle [G].

Details of all the known archaeological/historical sites in Cornwall can be examined by appointment during office hours at the Cornwall and Isles of Scilly Sites and Monuments Record, Cornwall Archaeological Unit, Cornwall County Council, Old County Hall, Station Road, TRURO TR1 3EX. Tel: Truro (01872) 323603. Fax: (01872) 323804.

ISBN 0906294 21 5   © Cornwall Archaeological Unit 1990, 1993, 1997
Twelveheads Press, Chy Mengleth, Twelveheads, Truro, Cornwall TR4 8SN.